ENDORSEMENT

Brice Medlin is my friend and a genuine seeker of the truth of the Kingdom of God and how to live it authentically in this world. He is caught in the middle and has a father who mentored him well by his life. His story will touch you with a deep awareness of gratitude for a man who struggles to be real in his response to God and people made in His image. Thank you, Brice, for inviting us into your story written well from the heart.

Terry S. Smith

CAUGHT in the MIDDLE

by: j. brice medlin, ii

AUTHOR ACADEMY elite

Caught In The Middle © Jack Brice Medlin, II. All rights reserved.

Printed in the United States of America

Published by Author Academy Elite
PO Box 43, Powell, OH 43035
www.AuthorAcademyElite.com

All rights reserved. This book contains material protected under international and Federal Copyright Laws and Treaties. Any authorized reprint or use of this material is prohibited. No part of this book may be reproduced or transmitted in any form or by any means, electronic or mechanical, including photocopying, recording or by any information storage and retrieval system, without express written permission from the author.

Identifiers:
LCCN: 2020904686
ISBN: 978-1-64746-194-2
ISBN: 978-1-64746-195-9
ISBN: 978-1-64746-196-6

Available in paperback, hardback, e-book, and soon to follow audiobook

All Scripture quotations, unless otherwise indicated, are taken from the Holy Bible, The Living Bible copyright © 1971. Used by permission of Tyndale House Publishers, a Division of Tyndale House Ministries, Carol Stream, Illinois 60188. All rights reserved.

Any Internet addresses (websites, blogs, etc.) and telephone numbers printed in this book are offered as a resource. They are not intended in any way to be or imply an endorsement by Author Academy Elite, nor does Author Academy Elite vouch for the content for these sites and numbers for the life of this book.

Book cover by Debbie O'Byrne @ Jetlaunch
Book edited by Kimberly Thurow and one other.

DEDICATION

It is easy to whom I will dedicate this book. During the writing of this book, my father took a turn for the worse and died. He found out last year that he had liver cancer. He worked hard and beat the cancer. Just a short two months prior we celebrated his being cancer free as announced by his doctor. Then on a Sunday morning I saw my sister's name pop-up on my phone. Immediately my reaction was "Dad". Two days later he was in a hospice facility and by Friday, he was gone. I still can't believe it is possible. I have worked in the medical field for years and know there are chances. However, it will always be a question in my mind. How is a person cleared of a disease and then die of the very disease of which they have been cleared just two months later? He was not only the father we all long for in this world, but he was my primary editor of this book. I remember when I sent him the introduction and first chapter of this book. He was so proud of me and looked forward to the rest of the book. He read the first chapter and called me saying "I never knew you had gone through your own personal Hell." He was unaware of all the hardships that I had been through. He is my rock and has always been consistent. It is because of him that I have undertaken the desire to write this book. While the world around us dictates our moralities, God stays the same. Dad always stayed the same. What he said once was the same always. If I was writing the book of Hebrews, it would include his name in the chapter of the "heroes of Faith." One thing that can be said about Jack Brice Medlin I, "he is now seeing firsthand what he has always believed in." I will miss the almost nightly phone conversations. May this book have half the impact that my Dad had on people. He always said, "Nothing is more important in life than human beings and their souls". Until I see you again this book is dedicated to you and your memory. I love you Dad!

CONTENTS

Introduction ix

Chapter 1: My Story 1

Chapter 2: The Pendulum 31

Chapter 3: The Defense 45

Chapter 4: Is There A Hell 67

Chapter 5: The Sex Stuff 91

Chapter 6: Down To The River 103

Chapter 7: The Stuff Not Talked About 113

Chapter 8: The Political Chapter 123

Chapter 9: The Sum Of All Things 141

Chapter 10: My Psalms 155

INTRODUCTION

"Why don't you write a book?" they said. Something I never thought I would do. In fact, English has always been my weak subject. My father has written books, but I never thought it would be me. There are many roles that we do not mean to or think we will do, but God calls us to serve in them. It was not my intention to be president of the HOA where I live, but I saw what was happening to the property. So, on the board I went and now have been elected president. It is the same reason that I have decided to write this book. This book is not something that I dreamed of or thought would come to fruition, but here it is. I have lived enough days and experienced enough life to see things that are troubling.

Some of the beliefs are not new. They are problems that were addressed in the various letters written to the early church. Yet there is a resurgence of some of these beliefs. Other beliefs are new because of the society in which the church is involved today. People who follow Christ are to be "set apart" from the world. Instead we are letting the world define who God is or who the world thinks he should be. We are also letting the world define what is moral (if any) and immoral. For instance, you have a bill in the state of California that states you cannot preach that alternative lifestyles are a sin. There are also demonstrations at churches in cities because they preach against alternative lifestyles. This is just a sample of what is happening and it is just the beginning. The LOVE that God has shown us is beyond anything we deserve. He has done immeasurable things for us, which this book will hopefully convey. It kills me to see humans redefine his love to fit their personal feelings or fit the philosophies of the day or a political agenda. It all started one day when I was asked "why do you believe there is a Hell." The question took me by surprise. Are you serious? At first I was going to call this book "A Two-way Street." Not much later I

INTRODUCTION

was in a discussion with another person who believed salvation was earned based upon how many people you have dunked (baptized). It was crazy and wanted to make me pull my hair out. No wonder people are leaving Christianity in droves. Of course, there are several reasons for the decline. I have no doubt that this is one reason that people are leaving and outside people are looking inward and thinking that they do not want any part of this thing called Christianity. Hence the change in title names to what it is now.

This book is not meant to be political. Although the prevailing philosophies of the day have a big influence on how we interpret scripture. In fact, it is impossible to not let our politics of the day effect the way we worship God. Liberalism and Conservatism have turned the Bible and Jesus' message into a circus. This book is being written because of the extreme views not only in politics, but also to show how these views develop and determine our beliefs of scripture. As we are fed propaganda every single day in the news, tv, or movies we watch, so, too, we are fed propaganda by various groups that call themselves "christian." At the time of the writing of this book, a high level person in the

FBI has been fired. How many of you that watch the news believe that he is losing his pension? The truth is, this person is NOT losing the pension, only some benefits. By the way, did you know this person has a net worth of $11 million dollars? And their salary is only $200,000. I wonder how he or she accomplished that feat? However, you are being led by the media in a flat out lie. The same is true with your local news. Here, in Nashville, TN, we recently voted down a transit system with a $9 billion price tag. When the story first came out, the price tag was only $5 billion. (everyone knew it would cost more) The news quickly changed the price tag to $9 billion. As soon as the vote was over, the news lowered the price tag back to the $5 billion. Why? Now the local train system that we have, The Music City Star, just announced a reduction in services because of a safety system that is not on the trains. To fix it would cost $20 million. The news is quick to point out that the money to make the repairs was included in the bill that was voted down. As if it is the fault of the citizens of Nashville, TN that the Music City Star is having to downgrade its services. (the system is losing money anyway) Why is this cost not built into the operation

INTRODUCTION

of the train? There are numerous examples that could be used to show you the propaganda that you are fed EVERY day. The same is done with scripture. You can see how various verses are taken out of context and applied to whatever the subject matter is at hand. It cracks me up to see it be done by people that have left groups for doing the very same thing. Logic is such a rare thing these days. However, if it is a matter of the heart, rules and laws be damned. (That is a term that has no bearing on those that do not believe there is a Hell) It is a practice that has been going on though out history and it still goes on today. We have become such an extreme society that if you strive to be person in the middle, the left considers you cold and heartless and the right considers you a loose cannon. In fact, most people that read this are in denial and consider themselves to be in the middle. I guess this practice will go on until the end of time as long as humans are involved, but right now in my life, it seems intense. Most of the chapters in this book will only deal with subjects as they pertain to biblical matters.

    This book is not meant to be a scholarly tool. This is not going to be a boring topical discussion looking for the proper exegesis of each word. In fact, as I pen this book, I can see the reactions on both extremes. Both sides will condemn the things written within these pages. Rejection is what happens when you question the system. Only people who are searching for the mind of Christ will be open to possibilities. Many years ago, I worked in marketing and studied the KISS principle. The KISS principle is this, "Keep It Simple Stupid". Basically it means that the simpler the ad is, the easier it is for people to follow or remember. A good example of this is an ad I did for a photography studio. It was Easter time and the owner was taking pictures with bunnies. The ad I did was a simple bunny rabbit with his business name and phone number. I called a few days later to see how it was going and his appointment book was almost full. I believe that God believes in this KISS principle. In fact, have you ever noticed that scholars love to write books? Yet they write books and teach in schools, but they usually do not know how the real world works. Hence the books are written about what they don't teach people while they are in school. For instance, take prayer. How many lectures and books are there on "how to pray" yet it is so simple.

INTRODUCTION

Jesus gave us an example and what we do not know how to say the Spirit speaks for us. (Romans 8:26) God just wants us to talk to him. SO JUST PRAY! He will respond in one shape or form. Ever notice how our prayers are for a positive outcome. All we have to do is look or listen for the response. Despite what certain segments of population say. Hopefully you will look at this book as a "real world" book. Throughout the Old and New Testaments there are two commands: Love God and Love Others. I do not believe that God would make salvation something hard to understand that only the "learn-ed" people can truly disseminate. It is my hope that this book leads to more discussions of the subjects at hand. Also my prayers are for others to read this and be led to search for Christ. Please read with an open heart.

Let's get started.....

1
MY STORY

IN DECEMBER 1968 I opened my eyes for the first time. A little town in east Tennessee by the name of Greeneville, TN was my birthplace. You might be wondering why I am spending time telling my story. It is important that I present to you my background. You need to know where I came from so you see why I think the way I think. We think what we think because of several influences. Our childhood influences affect the way we think as adults. Parents, for those of us that have them, have a huge influence on our thinking. There is more on this later, but for now I want to share my story. It will include my younger years, my fall, and the recovery.

First is the early years. My father worked for the federal government in the early years. While I was born in Greeneville, TN, I only lived there for a year before my Dad was transferred to Atlanta, Georgia. This is where I grew up and spent most of my developing years. I had great friendships when I was a kid. One of my childhood friends still is a close friend and we now live within a couple of miles of each other. School wise I went to Fulton County public schools for most of my elementary years. My late elementary years, junior high, and high school years were at private schools.

I have fond memories of my years in Atlanta. There was one couple that were good friends with my parents. They were like adopted grandparents to me and my sister. He was a captain in the Atlanta Police department. That friendship allowed us to experience things that would have been difficult otherwise. Like going to the top of the Peachtree Towers to enjoy fireworks on the roof. Other events include going to the pre-opening celebration of the Hartsfield International Airport, riding in the squad car, and learning to stay out of the g&g (grass and gravel) when learning how to drive.

MY STORY

My father at some point ended up owning his own business. It was a chain of rehabilitation clinics. It was quite successful and gave us the opportunity to travel a lot when I was a kid. He was involved with the politics as well. I can remember doing my homework sometimes at the kitchen table of a very popular candidate that later became speaker of the house. This led me to become involved with the high school debate team and speech club. I was also involved with the choral group and even played the part of Scrooge in a high school play.

I was fortunate as a kid. My mom was a teacher out of college. Later she worked in the private sector. While my younger sister and I were growing up, she was a stay-at-home mom. She only worked once we were both in school and even then it was hours that allowed her to be home when we kids got home from school. My mom has passed on now due to Leukemia. My parents only lacked a week being married 49 years. Also on my mother's side of the family, my grandparents had a long lasting relationship. On my father's side, I just knew my grandmother. His father died of a massive heart attack when my dad was away in college. To the day that she died, my grandmother never got remarried.

Most people these days do not know what it is like to have marital relationships last so long or where they have a Dad and Mom that stay together.

Later in life my father started preaching as a labor of love. I say that because he did not do it for money. He loves people and more than that, he loves souls. Usually he preached for churches that were building up and really did not have the funds for a salary. That came later in life. Dad loved to carry his labor of love home with him. He would have sermons about this and that. Finally the family numbered his sermons at home. If a certain circumstance arose that required a sermon, he could just say "number 1" or whatever number was assigned to the sermon that corresponded with the event. It was a win-win situation. That way he did not have to use so much oxygen and my sister and I did not have to hear the full sermon that we already knew by heart.

December of 1985 was a huge time of change. During Christmas break of my junior year of high school, we moved from the big city of Atlanta, GA to the small town of Lebanon, TN. My Dad wanted to move his business at the time closer to family. The traffic was so bad in Atlanta that the change in the daily drive was going to be a delight. We lived in College Park and the school was in Norcross. For those of you readers that know the area, that is a long way. I made that commute during the construction of the "spaghetti" junctions. If you think the traffic is bad now in Atlanta, then you should have seen it when the connectors were cloverleafs. You would wait thirty minutes plus to go 2 miles. Needless to say, the move was a scary but welcome change.

I can remember the first day of school in Lebanon, TN. My fear was the attire that everybody would be wearing. The school was in the country and my biggest fear was everyone would be in coveralls. Fortunately my fears were put to rest and people were in regular clothes. The same is true for all of us. We have a preconceived idea how people are or their intellect based on their location, the clothes they wear, the car they drive, etc. The school was so much smaller than what I was used to. The teacher was writing my name on the chalkboard. He was spelling my name out B-R-I-C and before he could finish somebody hollered out "Brick?". There was laughter and the new name stuck.

It was not long before I had developed new friendships. There was no debate team or speech club. Instead I was encouraged to join the football team. The work outs really were good for my physical body. I did not see any playtime. That year was the final year that a local military academy would be open. Most of the seniors came to my high school. It greatly expanded the football team. Here I was with no experience, so I became a manager instead. Between living in a smaller town and so many friends that lived on farms, it was not long before I realized that there was "redneck" in my blood. It was a lot of fun living in a smaller town. There is a reason they call smaller towns the "heartbeat of America". So much can be missed when you live in a big city and so far away from your school. In Lebanon, I had a good time and formed some strong friendships that are still around today.

I graduated from high school in 1987. The eighties were a great time to grow up. America was in a positive point in the world. A lot of it had to do with Reagan being President and the end of what was known then as the global threat of nuclear war. The wall that separated East Berlin from West Berlin came down. Also

MY STORY

Russia ended Communism and started a transfer to a Democratic society. Life was grand. I had friends, good family, perceived peace in the world, and a happy church life. What more could you ask for.

Off to college for the next phase in life. I followed in my parent's footsteps and attended Freed-Hardeman University. It is a Christian college located in Henderson, Tennessee. My concentration of study was a business major. Without exception, you take a Bible class every semester. Attendance at a daily chapel service was also mandatory. Yearly, they have a Bible lectureship that brings people from different corners of the globe to study different Bible topics. Needless to say, you get you fair share of Bible studies. Do not misunderstand me, I have nothing but good things to say about the University. Many friendships were developed and fun was had. Just as there are those in society that we label as "elitists" so, too, are there some people in every walk of life that become experts in their fields and lose common sense. I became familiar with those that are "Bible elitists". On some days there was a late night game of cards in the dorm lobby where we would debate "scriptural authority".

One of the things that I participated in while at college was the University Chorus. I enjoy singing. We traveled extensively. These travels were primarily for admissions and fundraising for the university. Another reason though was to hopefully influence people to want to follow Christ. Pretty much every break from school was spent on a bus, as well as some nights and weekends. We spent the night in the homes of people that volunteered to keep us. On one trip I stayed in a home in Pensacola, Florida. I remember the home to this day. The couple had a son that was away in college. I met him some years later when I was on a trip and in a town above the Arctic Circle in Russia. This guy was on a team of people that were to follow a team with which I was traveling. He showed up ahead of the rest of his group because of his work schedule. One night we were up talking when he told me of his home in Pensacola, Florida. Come to find out, it was his house that I had stayed in and his parents that I had met. Talk about a small world.

After 2 years in college, I was bored with being a business major. I really liked science so that became my new major. Switching majors so late in my college career delayed my graduation by one semester. My graduation day came in December of 1991. Following graduation, I did what every kid does and moved back in with my parents. At that time in life, Dad was preaching full-time in Greeneville, TN. It was here that I studied for the MCAT and got a job at one of the local hospitals. My general practice doctor was the same doctor that helped me arrive in this world. It was fun seeing the notes that he had written back in 1968.

Several things happened in my years after college that bear mentioning. I will not draw these out and make this a long and boring chapter, but these are significant events that had a major impact on my life and led me to where I am today. Needless to say, I took the MCAT, but did not become a doctor. Instead, I got into marketing, although they call it "community relations" when you work in the medical field. Other things that happened was my trip to Vorkuta, Russia, a discovery class that I began teaching at church, and eventually matrimony.

In 1993, I had the opportunity to go to Russia. This was set-up as a medical/Bible teaching trip. It was just after the fall of Communism and we were all "friends."

Vorkuta is a city located above the Arctic Circle. I was there during the summer months when it never got dark. You just went by your watch when it was time to eat and sleep. There are many things that are stories on that trip, but there were awakening moments while I was there. How many of you remember the "food lines" to get food at the grocery stores that we were told in the media? There were "food lines" alright, but not for the lack of food. Those were the days that fresh cheese or other products arrived at the stores and they did not have as good of refrigeration that we do in this country. People were in line to get the produce while it was fresh. The smaller towns in Russia were several years behind America in those days. Later I was in a discussion with one of the locals, we were talking about the things we are taught in schools and on media about the other country. It was surprising to learn that they were not taught that the USA was their enemy. In fact, English was a second language that most of them spoke fluently. They were shocked to hear that we were taught they were our enemy and a danger to the free world. My eyes were opened on this trip that even in America are we fed an agenda by what we watch and read. It may or may not be true. That was my last trip across the pond.

Next came matrimony. I met this girl at work. We dated for a while and my Dad performed the ceremony. She was dunked and all was good. We lived in a small apartment that was formerly a barn. Once she finished school, we moved across town to a fancy neighborhood. Are we still married? No, but more on this later.

One other thing I did was teach an adult Bible school class at "church." It was a discovery class that looked at the various practices of the church. Basically a "why do we believe the things we believe" class. When you challenge your way of thinking, there are many things you can learn. It drives you to study things you have just accepted. The class went on for a while and some of the topics will be mentioned in this book. It was the most attended class at "church." I look back now and realize that some of the people were there to keep me in check and to make sure that I taught the things that were believed already. In fact, I can remember someone speaking up one day and saying "are you willing to risk your soul teaching this stuff." The answer came back "are you willing to risk your soul teaching stuff contrary to what you believe". It is very difficult to challenge what you think. Needless to say, the class ended when my disgrace came.

THE FALL

My life seems textbook up to this point. What is it they say, "wife, kids, and a white picket fence". I did not have any kids or the picket fence, but I thought I had a good life. Then it started hitting. First came my health. It was during this time that I had a long bout with stomach sickness. Hardly anything stayed down. Test after test was performed. There were scopes, x-rays, and blood tests and everything came back negative or borderline. This went on for months until I finally had an appointment with the chief surgeon and medical director of the hospital where I worked in psychiatry. He agreed to take out my gall bladder, but he was not sure that would be the answer. It was one of those things where the medical doctor says it is in your head and the head doctor says it is a medical condition. Well the gall bladder came out. The surgeon swears that he found a stone in the gall bladder, yet the path report came back negative. Who knows, maybe he was using Affirmation Therapy on me. Counseling followed and the pain was still there. Eventually it worked itself out and the pain has disappeared.

Then came my wife's health. She, too, started to have similar symptoms. Once again, nothing could be found. The doctors did what they call an ERCP (Endoscopic Retrograde Cholangiopancreatography). That led to the rare condition of pancreatitis. This landed my wife in the hospital for a month. I learned one thing through this: always if at all possible, live on one income. That way there is the ability to handle all the bills if something happens to the other spouse. Living in that neighborhood was looking more and more like a bad thing. One of the doctors at the hospital felt sorry for us and donated a sizable amount of money. I felt really bad accepting the gift. We really needed the money, but never before had I ever accepted this form of generosity.

This led next to financial stress. Did you know that financial stress is among the top stresses in relationships? It is a goal now to live off one income if I ever marry again. It is amazing how many people live paycheck to paycheck. Then you add in trying to keep up with the Jones'. It was not long before everything started to add up and the stress played into the marriage. Both parties start not talking to one another. Down deep you probably blame the other spouse for the stress that you are going through. Then you start to wonder if the other spouse has feelings for you that they once had. A lot of relationships end up in affairs with other people at this point. For those that care, couples therapy is the course of action. Even then, it can wind up in divorce. Mine did. Even after months of couple's therapy, I came home one day to find it had been mostly emptied. I fell on the floor and remained there for a couple of days. A buddy of mine from my past work came by to check on me. He picked me up off the floor and took me to the bank. It was too late. The account was mostly drained.

No way was I able to afford the house. The mortgage was held by individuals. While it did not go on my credit, it was close friends and it was like we had been paying rent for the time we actually lived in the house. The house was just turned back over to the lien holders. As much as I hated it, the friendship was no longer an option. So where to live? At that time I did not have many options and I was not about to move back home. There was too much shame involved. It just so happened that the assistant medical director in the unit where I worked was moving. He did not want to leave his house empty and offered me to let me live in the basement of the house in exchange for keeping up the place until it sold. I was honored and gladly accepted. His basement alone was almost a castle. This was great living until his house sold. Then I was forced to rent a room in a house that belonged to a college student in town that I knew from the restaurant where we waited tables.

Next to fall was my business. It was in sales and marketing. The technology behind the product was sound. However, my dad, had been named the CEO of the main company behind the technology. Not long after, I remember getting the call. The company was involved in stock fraud. I had made the classic blunder and put all of my eggs into one basket. Never do that and if you have, diversify now. Literally I was flat broke and owed people money. There was nothing I could do, but cry. To get by, I started waiting tables at a fancy Italian place in town. I ended up being the interpreter that read all the immigration documents for those applying to live in the U.S. The family was all from New Jersey and New York. Mama loved me and she could barely speak any English. One time I was asked to navigate to a casino in the neighboring state. Mama showed me how to play slots. They even gave me a Sicilian name. I learned a lot working for them. When I left, I was told to call anytime I needed help. As they put it, "I was part of the family." Later I learned that being told that meant something more than just being a member of the family.

Just when you think it cannot get much worse, it does. The car that I drove was a fancy leased car. One day I rounded a curve to find someone in my lane. Without hesitation, I cut the person off next to me and did everything that I could to miss the other vehicle, but it was unavoidable. While it was not a head on collision, the other car went down my side. The other driver was driving on a suspended license and the car was not even his. Off to jail he went and the cops gave me a ride home, since they knew me from the restaurant. The kicker was when I made the call to the insurance. They

MY STORY

had canceled the wrong policy when I lost the house. Instead of canceling the home owner's insurance, they had canceled the auto policy. Here I was in a wreck and unbeknownst to me, I had no coverage. I was paying a lease on a car that was unable to be driven and was going to cost a lot of money to fix. Fortunately dad had an older car that was not being driven back home. It needed new tires and an oil change, but other than that was good to go.

I was miserable and ashamed. It was like the whole world had come crashing down around me and there was nothing I could do. It was the worst thing I had happen to me. There was anger everywhere. I was mad at the world. More than that there was anger at God for letting all this happen. Because of the way I was brought up, I figured there was no hope for me and my soul. I cut off almost all of my relationships. There had to be a better way so that this scenario did not happen again.

THE RECOVERY

They say "that time heals all wounds". I disagree with that statement. A wound may cover itself, but it never really "heals". Scar tissue forms over the wound and every now and then you feel the pain or discomfort that was associated with the wound. My healing took several years and really is still happening. There is no set length of time to get over something. Most textbooks say at least a year, but each person is different. Mine has taken several years, and I am still working on recovery. The three major areas that I have worked on for recovering are relationally, financially, and spiritually.

One night during that time, my best friend suggested that I move to Nashville, TN. My best friend and I are life-long friends. We have known each other since the age of two years old. Our parents were friends in Atlanta, GA and my friend and I were the same age. Since then, we have lived miles apart, but we have always remained in contact. Even now we live about a mile apart and have lived as close as a few doors down from each other. Those type of friendships are few and far between. It took some time, but I made the move.

I came to Nashville, TN in May of 2001. I did not come alone. At the time I was dating someone that also wanted a change. We also lived together which is shock and unbelievable to people that I grew up around. Yes,

MY STORY

we know the statistics for people that live together, but we also know the stats for current marriages that succeed or don't succeed. This lasted for a few years. It all changed when her Dad died and her brother later committed suicide. Her mother had been dead several years. I found out later that she had been funneling money into a separate account to go out on her own. She left at this point and to this day, I have not had any contact with her. There was one contact when I bought a condo. She had boxes in our storage that belonged to her father. I still had an email for her and she showed up to get those boxes. There was another guy in the car and a kid. I can only imagine what happened when we separated. It only adds to the wall around my heart.

I had another vice that I took up during this time. It started out as one beer a night because it would put me to sleep. That developed into full-fledged drinking. I was never an alcoholic per se, but I drank a lot. I do not know if it was a phase that everyone goes through or if it was my crutch for what all I was going through. I became an expert drink maker as well. I can make some killer martinis and margaritas. It all ended when I won 2nd place for desserts in the Music City BBQ

Fest. I got smashed that night. It took 3 days to get over that hangover. The room just kept spinning. My cousin brought over some Diet Coke and salty potato chips so I could eat. I do not recommend these items for hangovers, but for this time, it worked and allowed me to eat. During this time I asked God to get me through this and it would never happen again. My co-workers laughed and said "till the next time". It stuck with me and a promise is a promise. I have never lost control since and now I hardly touch the stuff. Not because I think it is wrong, but because it has gotten to where my body doesn't react well to alcohol as I age. It doesn't work for everybody. Some need AA, but for me, it was a decision to stop getting drunk on alcoholic drinks and a pact that was made with God. So, for me, it was a matter of mind over matter and I just stopped.

My biggest piece of advice is too not feel pressured by friends and family. Many people will offer advice and they all have something to say. Even now, I am pressured to get married. They even tell me what type of person I need to marry. Unfortunately, the right person has not come along and it will take a lot for me to let the wall down. I still have not remarried. The pain is so much and I keep comparing current relationships to my failed one, that I have built a wall around my heart which makes it hard to have any meaningful relations. Looking back, I have lost relationships because of it. You want things just to be normal and just be friends, but the other party wants more. One day you look back and have lost touch with that person because they have moved on. All because you didn't make a move.

One side effect through all of this is a lack of trust in all humans. It started in 2001, when I moved to Nashville, TN. I was living in an apartment then. It was a haven of stray cats mainly because people had put them out when they found out that they were going to have them added to the rent in pet deposits and monthly fees. My neighbors noticed that I was able to win the hearts of even the most skittish cat. I was told that an animal knows a person's heart. Later I started putting out food and found that cats talk when there is free food.

It was a brutally cold winter, so I borrowed a large cage from a local cat rescue lady. I would bring the cats in at night and then put them out the next morning when I left for work. One night a Siamese cat just came on in and got comfortable. Later I found out she was an "apple head" Siamese and rare. She hated going out in mornings and would hide. My heart went out to her and that led me to adoption.

Before I adopted them and took two in, they got pregnant. At one time I had 12 cats and knew that I needed help. That led me to the Nashville Cat Rescue and started my side career. Some kittens were adopted and some stayed with me after failed adoptions. I worked with the Nashville Cat Rescue for several years. As a volunteer, I cleaned cages at the adoption center and used my marketing skills to get them setup at Oktoberfest in town to raise money and get furrever homes for kittens and cats. One role that I had with the cat rescue is as Santa Paws. I have become known around town as "Santa Paws" and take pictures with animals to raise money.

A funny story that happened to me when I first got into animal rescue. I mentioned that they were pregnant. The one cat was obviously pregnant. The Siamese cat got bigger, but was not so obvious. One night, the Siamese was having convulsions. Of course, it was a weekend night when nothing is open except the emergency pet clinic. I loaded her in a carrier and off we went. That night was quiet in the clinic, so the problem with the cat was quickly identified. The carrier was on top of the counter while I filled out the paperwork. Then there was a "meow". Now the cat was new to me, but I knew her "meow" and it didn't sound like her's. The clerk looked in the carrier, then at me and said "she's having kittens". Like I didn't know. I felt dumb. They took her to the back and assisted her deliver the kittens. It was nice that they did the service and did not charge me. Normally these emergency clinics charge you money for walking through the door. Anyway, the cat(s) and I made it home.

 All people suffer financially from divorce, but it was mentioned earlier that I had a business crash as well. Between paying for the divorce, the loss of the house, the loss of the car, and the business failure, I was beyond broke. Lawsuits followed. I owed lots of money and now had to pay an attorney to represent me. Most of my debt was written off as bad debt. Sometimes the attorney would be busy and send me to court to talk with the opposing attorney. I learned a lot about the legal system. It takes a long time to settle some cases.

I got frustrated one time and called my attorney to express my dissatisfaction. He told me that the longer it took, the better it was for me. He said it was not like wine and did not get better with age. It took some time, but everything was settled and I was blessed to have the cash to pay for the settlements. There had to be a better way.

Once again my best friend came through. At his invitation, I joined a financial class. The director that developed this process, did so from going through his own financial hard times. I saw him at a book signing one time. I told him that I credited Jesus with saving my soul and him with saving my life. His process and rules changed every fabric of my being. It is not easy changing at first, but two years into the new way of living, I realized that credit was a thing of the past. Once you get used to budgeting and used to living on the cash you have on hand, your life will be different. For some reason, people fear the "B" word. So many people associate a budget with having no money to play with on the weekends or to travel. There will be some lifestyle changes, but your life will be less stressful. I even bought a house with no credit score. It is possible.

MY STORY

Besides learning how not to live paycheck to paycheck, I have also learned to live within my means and have an emergency fund.

The class teaches one the laws for collections as well. Did you know that there are certain things that these companies can and can't say and there is a statute of limitations on debt collecting? There have been times that this part of the class has been very handy. The lawsuits eventually stopped and things settled down, but every now and then a collection letter comes in the mail for an old debt that was sold off by the original lender. The things I learned in this class got me through these times. If you have not taken this class, I recommend you do. It can change your life. The director takes something that seems complex and shows how simple it really is. If you are like me, there will be an anger phase you go through to your parents, schools, etc. for not teaching you this stuff at an earlier age.

The spiritual recovery is the hardest. There is a desert that most people go through. Some people make it and some don't. For Jesus it lasted 40 days, but mine lasted longer. Sometimes we make our desert wanderings longer than they need to be. When I relocated to

Nashville, I started working at a local moving company. I would literally show up and sit on a bench and wait to see if I was chosen to work that day. One thing led to another and I eventually became a qualified driver for the company. This allowed me a lot of time to think while I was on the road. Before I became self-employed I was a manager in the company and was there for eighteen and 1/2 years before I left. There are three main things that happened that have helped me in my quest. Those things are sayings by a preacher, the answer to my question of "why", and a man named Terry Smith and his company called Coaching: Life Matters.

Every now and then a preacher can say something that sticks with you. While I do not remember the exact day or time, I do remember the saying. "God has thick shins and expects a reaction." Wow!! It hit me like a boulder. I had not realized it until that day, but I was angry at God. They say you are not supposed to get angry at him, but I was very angry for all that I was going through. It is alright to be angry at God because he has the power to make all of the suffering in this world just go away with a word. Right? They say "admittance is the first step". I had been denying it, but I was angry at God and that was my admittance.

Once I admitted being angry with God, it led to the next step. I had to answer the question of "why". Why had God allowed all of this stuff to happen? There are books written about this subject. There is no easy answer and most of us are faced with having to answer that question. Like I said earlier, I had a lot of time on the road by myself to think. Eventually I answered the question for me. The answer is different for everybody and takes different amounts of time to answer the question. The answer for me was that this started with the fall. It is an imperfect world and the rain falls on the just and the unjust alike. (Matt. 5:45) It really is not God's fault. He created the world perfect and mankind messed it up. Yes, he could step in and stop it, but that would take away our freedom of choice. Freedom of choice is a very important phrase that will show up again later in this book.

Have you ever had your story done? I first met Terry Smith in a class called "Discovering Yourself" in 2001. It was a class that utilized the genogram to tell you why you do the things that you do. I learned a lot from the class, but not immediately. It took several years, but it finally took. In January of 2012, Terry asked me to come by his office. Something kept nagging at me and I eventually agreed. We did my story and this time the purpose was to show where God had been active in my life. He is part of a group called "seekers" and he invited me to be a part of the group. For many years I met with this group. Terry has some mottos I picked up. Most notably are, "children are the best recorders and worst interpreters", "we best understand God when we feel it in our head, heart, and gut", and "there is nothing more important than a human being." It is a wonderful thing when you see how God has been active in your life. That is what Coaching: Life Matters does and you can have your story told as well. I credit Terry with bringing me back to reality. Most importantly, he has a way of showing you grace and what it can do for you no matter what your past or current situation.

 I cannot say enough for what Terry Smith means to me. It is he who brought me back from the brink. He and his wife are the kindest people you have ever met. Terry likes to write haiku poetry. It is his influence that taught me to start writing mine. Several are in the

MY STORY

back of this book for your enjoyment. I may not be at 100%, but God's grace puts me over that percentage. He can for you as well.

Whether your story is better, same, or worse, it doesn't matter. Grace is a wonderful gift. It has the power to cover a multitude of flaws. I did not know what God's love was, but it was shown to me. Hopefully this book will do the same for you. Now you know my story and how it has influenced me. Now you know why I think the way I think.

2
THE PENDULUM

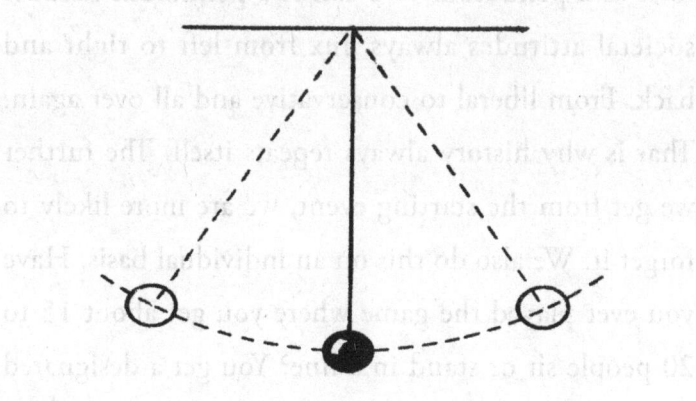

"Back and forth it goes,
Where it stops,
Nobody knows."

"Major Bowes Original Amateur Hour"

THE SAYING IS usually "round and round", but for our purposes here it is back and forth. It denotes life on an individual scale and a national scale. We spent a lot of time in the last chapter telling you about me. We detailed what all has happened to me to affect the way I think. Now it is time to tell you why you think the way you think.

Life is a pendulum. There is a long psychiatry term for the actual event, but to make it easy, we will refer to it as a pendulum. We call it a pendulum because societal attitudes always flux from left to right and back. From liberal to conservative and all over again. That is why history always repeats itself. The further we get from the starting event, we are more likely to forget it. We also do this on an individual basis. Have you ever played the game where you get about 15 to 20 people sit or stand in a line? You get a designated person to tell a phrase to a person at one end of the line. The phrase is told quietly to the next person in line. You then have the person at the other end of the line to repeat the phrase word for word for what it was at the beginning of the line. What you find is that it is totally different. If this happens on such a small scale, you can imagine what happens on a big scale.

Take, for a recent example, the United States. We come back from WWI. Life is great and a party, i.e. the roaring 20s. We think it is all over and life is grand. Then the great depression happens. What a shock!! A lot of people are broke and losing everything. There are people in the cities that temporarily give their kids to relatives out in the country just so they can have something to eat. Then you have WWII and rationing. A far cry from what it was in the United States after WWI. Needless to say, it was liberal then things switched to conservative. You can still tell people that lived during that time. The sayings go like this, "You better clean your plate", "eat what is put before you", or "eat now cause you don't know when you will eat again". They have been through it and know how it is to not have plenty. Since the 60's, America has been in a liberal mode. That is currently changing. That is why the liberals are kicking and screaming.

It also happens on an individual basis. Usually it follows a trauma in one's life. Everyone remember a certain late night host? He was the last of the funny late night talk show hosts. The late night shows now have ceased to be funny at all. These guys think they are funny, but they fool themselves. For the longest time I used to watch this host. Then it all changed when this person had heart surgery. They say it changes you and for him it did. At that point there was a change. I tried to give him a little time, but it didn't do any good and I quit watching the show. The same thing happens to you. I can't count how many people, couples specifically, where one gets sick and the attitudes change. You may be as conservative as they come, but your spouse gets sick and it changes you. You may not be liberal, but you will start spouting liberal ideas. It is just a part of life. Back and forth we swing.

We are all BIGOTED!! Bet that got our attention and it is true! This word has such a negative connotation because it is usually associated with race, but that is not the definition of this word.

big·ot

'bigət/

noun

noun:**bigot**; plural noun:**bigots**

1. a person who is intolerant toward those holding different opinions.

When I say that we are all bigoted, I mean it and can prove it to you. Do you have kids? I bet you think they are an angels. What sports team do you cheer for? Then you have the two things you never bring up at big family dinners. Do you vote Republican or Democrat? Where do you go to church and what do they believe there? I can go on and on, but you get my drift. If someone disagrees with certain statements you believe are right and true, they are the bigot, not you. As my father's saying goes, "we all seek truth until it disagrees with what we believe."

Let's start with your kids. If you have kids, we all want the best for them. We will do anything to protect them. Now, I don't have human kids, but my fur babies are everything to me. I pray to God that nothing happens to my kids. I can't imagine what I would do if something bad happened to them. You probably feel the same regarding your kids. Sometimes they step in it. Despite all of our efforts to make sure our kids stay in "the straight-and-narrow", they still mess up. Worst case scenario, they lose their life. How devastating! The saying goes, "a parent should never out live or bury a child." The number of marriages that have failed due to a child loss is extremely high. Once again, as well with finances, here comes the blame game. Back to the point, you are at the funeral and no matter if they are major gang bangers. They are all angels, and they may be, no matter what they have gotten involved in and you better not disagree.

Where did you go to school? Are you a fan? Naturally we support our schools and their teams. We support our state teams because we live there. I am a fan of Tennessee volunteers. Why? I did not go to school there. I don't have any friendships there and I do not know anyone on the team. I grew up in the state of Georgia and should be a fan of that school. Instead, I follow Tennessee probably because I was born in that state and I live there now. However, I am a fair weather fan. I want teams to win. If they don't play well or have a losing record, I do not waste my time following the games. The point is I follow the team for no real reason.

Soon we go to the polls. You will punch the button or pull the lever for either the Democrat or the Republican. Have you ever thought about the reason you vote the way you vote? Is it because your parents voted that way? Today, the local news is a major reason why one votes the way they vote. Is it because of the way you were taught in school or your teachers voted a certain way? Although, what they teach is usually indicative of the way they vote. Maybe it is your friends or workmates that effect the way you vote. Peer pressure is strong even when we are past school. You don't want to hear the ridicule around the water cooler at work so you will vote the way they vote. The cliques form. Recently I went to my 30-year high school reunion and it was funny to see immediately how the old cliques from school reorganized. Nothing changes when it comes to mankind. Unless we will it.

The same thing applies to where we go to church. Why do you go there? Was it because your parents went there? When did you start? Do you ever pickup your Bible and read for yourself or are you just reciting everything you have heard the preacher and teachers say? Have you ever thought about these questions? I recently was in a discussion with someone about why they went to church where they go. The answer was that they had been to different churches with friends. That THAT is the way one tests their beliefs. Really? But, they all are right! That's why there is a building for every sect under the sun on each corner. You even have sects of sects that exist. More than that, you better believe and teach what they believe or else they end fellowship and we all want to belong. In a sense, some people use "church" as a social club.

So how can one not be bigoted in what they believe? Well, there is no way to be totally un-bigoted, but there is a way to eliminate most of the title. Simply have the facts to back up what you say. I said "facts" not hearsay or assumptions. In debate you have to have articles, etc. to back up what you say and the judge would then determine who made the better argument. The same can be done for any of the topics above or that comes up in your life. That is how you can be as little as a bigot as possible.

THE PENDULUM

Another word that describes all of us, and that we hate to be called, is "ignorant." All of us are ignorant about something, but the word makes us feel dumb. The definition of ignorance is:

ig·no·rant

lacking knowledge, information, or awareness about something in particular.

We can use the same items to talk about the term "ignorance". Let us say you have kids. To you, going through their life is so special. You try to do everything to protect them from the evils in this world. However, you find out that they have stepped in it. As much as we do not want them to hurt in any way, shape, or form, they have gotten themselves in pickle or worse, dead. A lot of the time it is because we do not want to believe it. We are therefore "ignorant" about our kid's behavior. Kids will be kids. It happens. One time, I can remember having a lock-in at the local YMCA. The adults were up playing cards and the kids were doing what kids do. I noticed a group of kids going into the racket ball court. It was dark, but I knew where the switch box was in the complex. The lights came on and lo and behold, kids. They were doing what kids do. One of them said to me, "how did you know?" My reply was "I was not born yesterday." Needless, to say, I was not ignorant to what kids do in that situation. Hopefully we are not at a funeral for our kid one day wondering how our kid got mixed in such a mess and we had no clue. Do not be ignorant about your kid(s).

You can go to school and still come out very ignorant. Tax payers spend more and more on education, yet the more ignorant are the students that we are producing. This is not limited to the public school systems, but also the private schools. I was in a conversation with a gentleman that had gone to one of the elite private schools. The discussion was about the types of world governments. It was amazing how much he did not know (ignorant) regarding the subject and of course he had been negatively influenced on the positives and negatives about each type. He was pretty sure that because of where he went to school, he was sure he was right. He put his trust in the professor's that he had studied under and not checked out what they had said.

THE PENDULUM

Like I said we are all ignorant about something. You cannot know everything about all things. You can also speak in ignorance as well. We are mostly parrots and recite the things we have heard and not checked out the facts. Recently it came out that there was a spy in a politician's campaign for the senate office. A video was released showing one of his aides saying "that Tennesseans are ignorant". While the statement is true that all people are ignorant about something, this statement was made about this politician saying they would vote "yes" for this candidate to be a Supreme Court justice. In other words, he just said it to get the votes of Tennesseans. Basically, he lied. So now we know if you vote for this person, you are no longer ignorant about what he says and you are voting for a liar. The aide that made that statement was ignorant about to whom he was speaking. He is no longer ignorant about spies in campaigns and he also still has a job, so it must reflect the view of the person he represents.

The same applies to what we believe the Bible says. How many times do we repeat what is said by a Sunday school teacher, a study book used, a prayer spoken, or verbiage used by someone in the pulpit. We trust them, so they must be speaking truthfully. One time, I was teaching a youth class and you always have to have a book to teach from, right? It was going well until I noticed the book was not teaching. Instead it was drawing conclusions that did not apply to the text in the Bible. We finally threw the book to the wayside and went strictly by the Bible. This was a text in a youth class. Imagine the other things that can be spoken in ignorance by well-meaning people all because they did not check out the facts before they spoke. Hebrews 5:13 and I Corinthians 3:1 refer to people as "babes" in Christ. This refers to people who are new to salvation. From salvation you rely on what others say as you grow into "adulthood". How sad to be misinformed or to stay in "childhood" all because you did not read the Bible on one's own. How many people are out there winning souls to Christ, but leave the souls feeding in infancy and do not appropriately add the "meat" to the diet.

If this book does anything, hopefully it causes you to get out your Bible and start reading it. Read it for the "first" time. Even if you think you have read the Bible numerous times, read it and think on your own. The Bible is a pretty good manual. There is everything in it to keep your attention. There is sex, politics, war, peace, family strife, etc. Pick the Bible up off the shelf and read it.

I can remember a discussion that happened one time when I worked on the Psychiatric ward in a hospital. One of the nurses was having a baby and the stories talked about were kids. The most positive thing discussed was "indoctrination". How great it was to have a kid so they could be taught to think like you think. How sad, but so true. If one is ignorant about a certain subject the likelihood of the offspring thinking erroneously about the same subject is almost guaranteed. This chapter has touched on only two words and there are others. We try to avoid these words in ourselves, but alas it is futile. The best way to avoid these words is to know the subject matter at hand. So pick up your Bible and get to studying.

3
THE DEFENSE

THERE IS A movie that I love to watch. In the movie, there is a lawyer that meets with a CIA guy in a bar and says the most profound statement. He guesses that the agent is German and admits he is Irish. He tells the agent "The only thing that makes us Americans is the rule book, the Constitution. Well, the only thing we have to go by is the Bible. The Bible could be said to be the Christian "rule book", but it is not a "rule book" as we know one. It provides us with the story of Salvation and how God's plan is meant for all. It is what Christians go by in this life. Without it we would just be lost.

Every now and then, it is necessary to go back to basics in the things that we do. In football it is blocking and tackling. Now it is time to go "back to basics" in Salvation. This chapter is called "The Defense" because of the events that occur in Acts, chapter 7. Here we have Stephen on trial for believing in Jesus as the Messiah. Notice what happens when you go against the established organizations. Power and positions are threatened. In chapter 6 the establishment even hires someone to tell lies about Stephen and that leads to his court appearance. Sound familiar? Not that anything

THE DEFENSE

happens like that today in our modern world where we are more civilized. Right? Anyway, back to Stephen. He is representing himself. In his defense of the charges he basically gives the history of the world from Abraham up to his time and it wasn't the movie version.

In Acts chapter 7 Stephen starts his defense:

> **1.** Then the high priest asked Stephen, "Are these accusations true?" **2** This was Stephen's reply: "Brothers and fathers, listen to me. Our glorious God appeared t our ancestor Abraham in Mesopotamia before he settled in Haran. **3** God told him, 'Leave your native land and your relatives, and come into the land that I will show you.' **4** So Abraham left the land of the Chaldeans and lived in Haran until his father died. Then God brought him here to the land where you now live. **5** "But God gave him no inheritance here, not even one square foot of land. God did promise, however, that eventually the whole land would belong to Abraham and his descendants—even though he had no children yet. **6** God also told him that his descendants

would live in a foreign land, where they would be oppressed as slaves for 400 years. **7** 'But I will punish the nation that enslaves them,' God said, 'and in the end they will come out and worship me here in this place." **8** God also gave Abraham the covenant of circumcision at that time. So when Abraham became the father of Isaac, he circumcised him on the eighth day. And the practice was continued when Isaac became the father of Jacob, and when Jacob became the father of the twelve patriarchs of the Israelite nation. **9** "These patriarchs were jealous of their brother Joseph, and they sold him to be a slave in Egypt. But God was with him **10** and rescued him from all his troubles. And God gave him favor before Pharaoh, king of Egypt. God also gave Joseph unusual wisdom, so that Pharaoh appointed him governor over all of Egypt and put him in charge of the palace. **11** "But a famine came upon Egypt and Canaan. There was great misery, and our ancestors ran out of food. **12** Jacob heard that there was still grain in Egypt, so he sent his sons—our ancestors—to buy some. **13** The second time they went, Joseph revealed his identity to his brothers, and they were introduced to Pharaoh. **14** Then Joseph sent for his father, Jacob, and all his relatives to come to Egypt, seventy-five persons in all. **15** So Jacob went to Egypt. He died there, as did our ancestors. **16** Their bodies were taken to Shechem and buried in the tomb Abraham had bought for a certain price from Hamor's sons in Shechem. **17** "As the time drew near when God would fulfill his promise to Abraham, the number of our people in Egypt greatly increased. **18** But then a new king came to the throne of Egypt who knew nothing about Joseph. **19** This king exploited our people and oppressed them, forcing parents to abandon their newborn babies so they would die. **20** "At that time Moses was born—a beautiful child in God's eyes. His parents cared for him at home for three months. **21** When they had to abandon him, Pharaoh's daughter adopted him and raised him as her own son. **22** Moses was taught all the wisdom of the Egyptians, and he was powerful in both speech and action. **23** "One day when Moses was forty years old, he decided to visit his relatives, the people of Israel. **24** He saw an Egyptian mistreating an Israelite. So Moses came to the man's defense and avenged him, killing the Egyptian. **25** Moses assumed his fellow Israelites would realize that God had sent him to rescue them, but they didn't. **26** "The next day he visited them again and saw two men of Israel fighting. He tried to e a peacemaker. 'Men,' he said, 'you are brothers. Why are you fighting each other?' **27** "But the man in the wrong pushed Moses aside. 'Who made you a ruler and judge over us?' he asked. **28** Are you going to kill me as you killed that Egyptian yesterday?' **29** When Moses heard that, he fled the country and lived as a foreigner in the land of Midian. There his two sons were born. **30** "Forty years later, in the desert near Mount Sinai, an angel appeared to Moses in the flame of a burning bush. **31** When Moses saw it, he was amazed at the sight. As he went to take a closer look, the voice of the Lord called out to him, **32** 'I am the God of your ancestors—the

God of Abraham, Isaac, and Jacob.' Moses shook with terror and did not dare to look. **33** "Then the Lord said to him, 'Take off your sandals, for you are standing on holy ground. **34** I have certainly seen the oppression of my people in Egypt. I have heard their groans and have come down to rescue them. Now go, for I am sending you back to Egypt.' **35** "So God sent back the same man his people had previously rejected when they demanded, 'Who made you a ruler and judge over us?' Through the angel who appeared to him in the burning bush, God sent Moses to be their ruler and savior. **36** And by means of many wonders and miraculous signs, he led them out of Egypt, through the Red Sea, and through the wilderness for forty years. **37** "Moses himself told the people of Israel, 'God will raise up for you a Prophet like me from among your own people.' **38** Moses was with our ancestors, the assembly of God's people in the wilderness, when the angel spoke to him at Mount Sinai. And there Moses received life-giving words to pass on to us. **39** "But our ancestors refused to listen to Moses. They rejected him and wanted to return to Egypt. **40** They told Aaron, 'Make us some gods who can lead us, for we don't know what has become of this Moses, who brought us out of Egypt.' **41** So they made an idol shaped like a calf, and they sacrificed to it and celebrated over this thing they had made. **42** Then God turned away from them and abandoned them to serve the stars of heaven as their gods! In the book of the prophets it is written, 'Was it to me you were bringing sacrifices and offerings during those forty years in the wilderness, Israel? **43** No, you carried your pagan gods— the shrine of Molech, the star of your god Rephan, and the images you made to worship them. So I will send you into exile as far away as Babylon.' **44** "Our ancestors carried the Tabernacle with them through the wilderness. It was constructed according to the plan God had shown to Moses. **45** Years later, when Joshua led our ancestors in battle against the nations that God drove out of this land, the Tabernacle was taken with them into their new territory. And it stayed there until the time of King David. **46** "David found favor with God and asked for the privilege of building a permanent Temple for the God of Jacob. **47** But it was Solomon who actually built it. **48** However, the Most High doesn't live in temples made by human hands. As the prophet says, **49** Heaven is my throne, and the earth is my footstool. Could you build me a temple as good as that?' asks the Lord. 'Could you build me such a resting place? **50** Didn't my hands make both heaven and earth?' (TLB)

First, Stephen presents God's relationship to man in three stages. There are actually more, but he just addresses the periods from Abraham. The first age is the pre-flood period. This includes the creation, the garden of Eden, and the fall. We have no indication how long this period lasts. For all we know, it was thousands of years. Then came the flood and the Patriarchal Age. In this age, the stories of God were passed down through the head of the family. Did you know that the flood is the most recorded event passed down through the ages? No matter what culture, there is a story of a flood in their history. We know the length of time of the flood to be forty days. Imagine not ever seeing rain before that time. Then you not only get the rain, but scriptures say "the waters erupted from the earth." (Gen. 7:11) Before this time, the earth was watered by a mist / springs. (Gen 2:6) The flood waters were on the earth for 150 years before the ark landed. (Gen 7:24) After the flood, eventually we have Abraham. The post-flood tells of Abraham all the way through the Moses and the 400 years of residence in Egypt. Moses performed signs and wonders before everyone to prove that God was God. All of this ended with the death of the first born males. Something to note here is that God put to death all of the firstborn males. The only people that were spared were the houses that were marked with blood of lambs. (Exodus 12:7) This closes the Patriarchal Age.

The next age that Stephen covers is the Israelite or Jewish Age. This age goes from Joshua to Jesus. Moses died in the wilderness. The next leader after Moses was Joshua. He led the Israelites into the promised land after the 40 years of wandering in the desert. It was in the desert wanderings that the tabernacle instructions were given. A place for God to reside among man. A direct symbol of God's desire to interact with mankind. Lots of things happened during the second age. Predicted by many was the coming of the Christ. He would issue in a new era. To the people in places of power this was a threat. All they knew was earthly power. There were many prophets that told of the next age coming, but many were tortured and died. Jesus came and performed signs and wonders. He was tortured and killed. Abraham even predicted that "if they won't listen to Moses and the prophets, they won't listen even if someone rises from the dead". (Luke 16:31) Notice that during his time on Earth, Jesus spent 40 days in the desert being tested by Satan. With all the "4's" being mentioned in the first and second ages, one might think that 4 is a significant number with God. It is my belief that most of us go through our own deserts. Some of us survive and come out on the other side. Unfortunately, some do not make it out of their own desert and remain there suffering, while others die. The death of Jesus marks the end of the second age and the beginning of the next age.

Next in Stephen's defense is the third age or the Messianic Age. This is the age that we are living in now. It began with the apostles as they were given charge by

Christ what we call "the great commission". In Matthew 28: 18-20 Jesus comes to his disciples as he is about to leave this world and says, I have been given all authority over Heaven and Earth. Therefore go and make disciples of all the nations, baptizing them in the name of the father and the son and the Holy Spirit. Teach these new disciples to obey all commands I have given you. And be sure of this: I am with you always even to the end of the age." How great Grace is, but we get stuck in Grace and are not taught the "weightier" things. (Matthew 23:23) This age is an expansion of the prior age. (Colossians 2:17) Each age is a foreshadow of the next age. The instructions of how to worship carry over to the next age. A good example of this is the veil that separated the Holy Place from the Most Holy Place in the temple. Only the high priest was allowed in the Most Holy Place. This veil was torn when Jesus died on the cross. No longer was there separation from God. He now resides in the tabernacle of the hearts of those who have faith in him. The second age had God residing in a building. Now the third age has God living in us. His kingdom is a spiritual kingdom and not tied to structures on this earth. Some of us mix-up the two ages. How many people do you know, maybe it is you, that think you must go to a building in order to worship God? How many of you know someone that thinks certain rooms in that building are places for God to reside? The kitchen needs to be separate and apart from the worship room. Sound familiar? The book of Hebrews is a good read to see how the Messianic Age is better that the Israelite Age.

Anyway, Stephen basically proclaims the end of the second Age and the beginning of the third age. This doesn't sit well with his judges. (those in seats of power under the current age) So Stephen does what any good lawyer does that has a winning argument going in a trial, He makes fun of the judges.

> **51** You stubborn people! You are heathen at heart and deaf to the truth. Must you forever resist the Holy Spirit? That's what your ancestors did, and so do you! **52** Name one prophet your ancestors didn't persecute! They even killed the ones who predicted the coming of the Righteous One—the Messiah whom you betrayed and murdered. **53** You deliberately disobeyed God's

law, even though you received it from the hands of angels." **54** The Jewish leaders were infuriated by Stephen's accusation, and they shook their fists at him in rage. **55** But Stephen, full of the Holy Spirit, gazed steadily into heaven and saw the glory of God, and he saw Jesus standing in the place of honor at God's right hand. **56** And he told them, "Look, I see the heavens opened and the Son of Man standing in the place of honor at God's right hand!" (TLB)

Once Stephen is making his closing arguments, the sentence is carried out:

57 Then they put their hands over their ears and began shouting. They rushed at him **58** and dragged him out of the city and began to stone him. His accusers took off their coats and laid them at the feet of a young man named Saul. **59** As they stoned him, Stephen prayed, "Lord Jesus, receive my spirit." **60** He fell to his knees, shouting, "Lord, don't charge them with this sin!" And with that, he died. (TLB)

So goes Stephen's trial and a brief history of the world up to this point. We do the same things even in this day and age. We don't like change and if something is said or a book is written that challenges what we already believe or the position we have in life, then we reject it. How many of us can do what Stephen did and when you are stoned, either literally or figuratively, and ask God not to "charge people with that sin?"

The age that is not included in Stephen's defense is what I call the Heavenly Age. This will be the age where God has gathered his flock in Heaven. The dead shall be raised and the living will be transformed. (I Corinthians 15:52) There will be a new Heaven and a new Earth. (Revelation 21:1) One of the most beautiful descriptions that I have heard of the afterlife involves a new Heaven and new Earth. Can you imagine what it will be like? We all picture the things that we dislike in this world. For some it is pain. We constantly hear "they are better off" when talking about a dead person. The experiences differ with that saying. When I worked in psychiatry, we would admit a lot of geriatrics that were dying of Alzheimer's. A debilitating disease for those that suffer and the caregivers. There were some that suffered with the disease so badly, they did not even know what planet they were on. They are definitely better off in the next age. We picture them having their minds again. I hate the loss that happens in this world. My question is will our animals be there? I am a big animal lover and pray that I see them again. We look forward to the next age with these images that we have in our minds. We know that it is promised, just how long do we have to wait? (Matthew 5:20)

Attached at the end of this chapter is a diagram that I made for a class when we talked about Acts 7. It is a visual of Acts Chapter 7 and what we have talked about. However, Stephen only knew the history of the world up to his time. A lot has happened to Christianity since then. After much persecution of Christianity came the time that started it as a state religion. then came Martin Luther and the Restoration Movement in Europe. This led to the discovery of America and the Reformation Movement. This in turn leads to all the different churches that are on every block and they all believe different things.

First followers of The Way were persecuted and they spread everywhere trying to find safety. If you have not read the book, you can read about all the people and their lives after the spread of the gospel. People were put on poles, soaked with oil, and lit on fire to light the streets. If you study the people that found anything important, you find most of them tortured, killed, or at the very least, their fortunes gone. Then in 306 A.D. - 337 A.D. came Emperor Constantine. He was the first to make Christianity a state religion. That stopped the persecution and began a power play by Constantine. He realized that if you control the religion, you control a large section of people. Hence all of this led to the Roman Church and at that time you better believe what they believed or you would die. Constantine even had meetings in Nicea, Turkey. Appropriately called "The Council of Nicea". You might be surprised that it is in Turkey, but Istanbul, Turkey used to be called "Constantinople". Yep, you guessed it! Built by Emperor Constantine. Here at these meetings a group of people determined what was going to be in the Bible and how to practice it. You mean there are more books than what is in the Bible? Once again, yep!! You can see how the Roman Empire and the Council of Nicea played a major role in our practices today.

The next big thing to happen is Martin Luther, the invention of the printing press, and the Restoration Movement. Martin Luther lived from 1483 to 1546. He was a professor in the town of Eisleben, Saxony (which is a part of Germany now). On October 31st, 1517 Martin nailed a document to the church door of 95 theses. He, along with a few others, had been questioning several of the practices of the state-run church. Normally you would be labeled as a "heretic" and killed for doing such a thing, but the state-run church had another problem to deal with at the time. The invention of the printing press. In 1454, the printing press put out a translation of the Bible. That was a major problem for the Roman Church because everyone was then able to read the text for themselves. Before this, you were told what to believe and it was accepted. In a sense, we do this today. Instead of reading the entire Bible, we trust the man in the pulpit or teachers to divine what we believe. This led to the Reformation Movement. There was a major power shift from the Roman Church to the individual countries at the time. Sure, there were some groups formed that just disagreed with the teachings of the Church, but some groups were started out of power to their governments. An example would be the _____ Orthodox Church. You can fill in the blank with most western and some eastern European country names at the time and it will fit.

Many branches broke off from the main Church at the time. This would include a group of Puritans. They got together and got on a ship, named "The Mayflower". Bound for a new land to worship the way that they wanted. This eventually led to the Restoration Movement in America. It was an attempt to get back to the Bible. There were many groups that divided over the attempt to get back to New Testament worship. Between the groups that formed from the Restoration Movement and the one's that formed out of the Reformation Movement, you now have buildings with names on them on every street corner. The Restoration Movement stopped with the groups named "Disciples of Christ, the Christian Church, and the Church of Christ. Some of them claim to be non-denominational, but they are perceived as denominational. They may not have central offices, but they do have their college campuses that dictate what should be taught. I would know. I went to one of their colleges. The Restoration Movement is now dead. Too many have left the ideals on which the Restoration was founded. They still do good deeds, but they have turned the church into social clubs that want your membership. It is still a money game for some. The bigger they are, the more money they have to build a bigger building. The preacher is a paid leader and most of the membership sits in the pews on Sunday's and expects the select few to do all of the work. The Restoration Movement should not be dead and there is a lot to do still. Now we try to be accepted by everyone and whatever you do, no judging. This includes the belief that people can worship or live the way that they want as long as you believe in Jesus.

There are pockets of people in all groups that strive for the heart of Jesus. This book in no way, shape, or form is going to be a condemnation of the way worship is done. It will look at various issues that may affect one's worship, but the main goal is to get the reader of this book to also read (as if it were the first time) the Bible.

THE DEFENSE

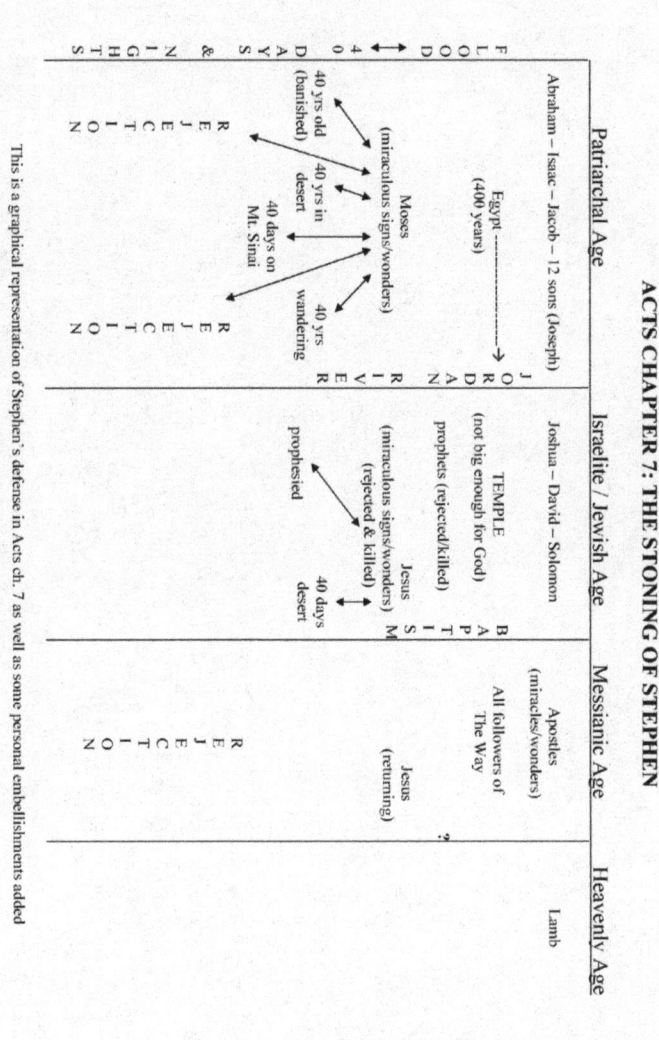

ACTS CHAPTER 7: THE STONING OF STEPHEN

Patriarchal Age	Israelite / Jewish Age	Messianic Age	Heavenly Age

Abraham – Isaac – Jacob – 12 sons (Joseph)

Joshua – David – Solomon

Egypt (400 years) → JORDAN

Moses (miraculous signs/wonders)
- 40 yrs old (banished)
- 40 yrs in desert
- 40 days on Mt. Sinai
- 40 yrs wandering

RED SEA & REJECTION

TEMPLE (not big enough for God)

prophets (rejected/killed)

Jesus (miraculous signs/wonders) (rejected & killed)
- BAPTISM
- 40 days desert
- prophesied

Apostles (miracles/wonders)

All followers of The Way

Jesus (returning)

REJECTION

Lamb

FLOOD
0 ↔ 4
DAYS & NIGHTS

This is a graphical representation of Stephen's defense in Acts ch. 7 as well as some personal embellishments added

- mankind messes up every age from Garden of Eden on because we reject God
- water is involved before each new beginning
- the number "4" is a key number in scripture

4
IS THERE A HELL

NOW WE COME to the chapter that is the original reason that this book was written. In fact, it is important more than ever to write this book, as the philosophy contained in the next few pages becomes more and more vocalized. It has even been proclaimed by the person that a lot of people look to for their religious guidance. It all started awhile back when I was sitting in a very small group. We were having a small Bible study when this philosophy was mentioned. I disagreed with the stated position and was asked "Why do you believe in your position". It has since spread or maybe my eyes have been opened as to the philosophy and I see it in a lot of places. There are some positions that are vocalized with regard to one's belief's that have a minimal effect. However, there are some that have a direct impact on the souls of people. These positions need to be addressed and stopped before they are allowed to spread. The position which I am referring to is "there is no Hell". It is believed by a lot of people in all walks of life and it needs to be stopped in its tracks or "nip it in the bud" as us Southern folks refer to it. The military refers to it as "neutralizing the threat". It is a cancer that is spreading and needs to be treated early. It is a philosophy that is dangerous in the way it leads those that supposedly believe the Bible to be the word of God.

One school of thought is there is no Hell. You can do anything you want because there is Grace to go around. This is a mutation of a philosophy that I dealt with in my younger days. That is the "once saved, always saved" crowd. Just after college I was living at home and I called another preacher in a different denomination in town. I asked him if he would be willing to meet to discuss the "once saved, always saved" belief. He reluctantly agreed. I just wanted to hear why one would believe in this teaching. The main thing was that I was there to listen. It was hard over-coming the fact that I was a preacher's son in town, but he agreed to meet. There were three people at the meeting. I guess he felt threatened, but I was just there to listen. One thing about that teaching is that those that believe in it run to the book of Ephesians. Ephesians 2:8,9. It is a gift of God. Therefore there is nothing that we need to do to get it. It just covers everyone period. This is one school of thought.

The other school of thought out there goes to the other extreme. It goes to the side where what you do gets you points. The more points that you have collected, the better your chances for getting accepted into Heaven. This argument bases your salvation on works.

The same thing is promoted by several groups out there. You have to be perfect to get into Heaven. The more souls you win the more chances you have in your pocket when you get to judgment. This puts people in a position of undue stress. In fact, a lot of people think there is no chance, so they just give up all together. How sad that our salvation is on either "no accountability" or so stressful it makes you not to want to try.

There has to be a different way. You have Grace that allows one to live however they want and on the other side you have all works. So, let's look at this subject and see what we find. On a side note, anyone know where the term "Christian" came from? We know that people were first called "Christians" in the town of Antioch. This is explained in the book of Acts 11:26. It is kind of like me being called a "trekkie" because I happen to be a fan of all things "Star Trek". I once went to a show and realized that I was not the fan that I thought I was. Did you know that some people actually have learned and speak an alien language? Now that is fandom. If only more people were into the Bible that much. Anyway, they were called "Christian" based on the name of the person they were teaching, Jesus Christ. However, it wasn't a name that you wanted to be called. It was a derogatory name that has stuck, but the teachings of Christ were not popular back then. People that followed his teaching were instead called followers of "The Way". (Acts 9:2) Maybe we need to go back to being "followers of The Way" instead of "Christian" since "Christian" is so broad a word nowadays. Followers of The Way went through their own Hell on earth so that we have the freedoms we have today.

Anyway, enough of the side sermon and back to the subject at hand. I mentioned in the Introduction how this book came about. First off, the facts are scientific ones. Sir Isaac Newton developed his Third Law of Thermodynamics. If you are into physics, it goes like this, "for every action there is an equal and opposite reaction." Let's take a cannon for example. The reason for the recoil of the cannon is the Third Law of Thermodynamics. That is why the cannons are built so heavy and tough, so there is a lot of friction when the ball is fired out of the opened end. For every good hero, there is the opposite villain from which to keep us safe. You do not have to look far to see the example. The new hero movies have great examples of this. In today's movies they all have similar gifts, but they choose sides. The good versus the evil. We all love a hero. It is where we get the saying "good always triumphs over evil." There is a war on earth. God and the Devil are fighting for our hearts at a regular interval. It is a spiritual warfare that we don't see physically. But sometimes we see it and live it.

The Bible is very specific when it describes Satan and Hell. Even Jesus saw Satan cast from Heaven. Luke 10:18 states that Satan "fell like lightning when he was cast out of Heaven. Satan is described as the most beautiful of all angels and was going to be God's main helper. (Ezekial 28:14) The Bible is specific about Hell being created by God for Satan and his followers. (Matt.25:41) We know that those that are lost go to a very hot place. In Luke 16 there is a parable that Jesus tells that describes Hell.

[19] Jesus said, "There was a certain rich man who was splendidly clothed in purple and fine linen and who lived each day in luxury. [20] At his gate lay a poor

man named Lazarus who was covered with sores. ²¹ As Lazarus lay there longing for scraps from the rich man's table, the dogs would come and lick his open sores. ²² "Finally, the poor man died and was carried by the angels to sit beside Abraham at the heavenly banquet. The rich man also died and was buried, ²³ and he went to the place of the dead.

There, in torment, he saw Abraham in the far distance with Lazarus at his side. ²⁴ "The rich man shouted, 'Father Abraham, have some pity! Send Lazarus over here to dip the tip of his finger in water and cool my tongue. I am in anguish in these flames.' ²⁵ "But Abraham said to him, 'Son, remember that during your lifetime you had everything you wanted, and Lazarus had nothing. So now he is here being comforted, and you are in anguish. ²⁶ And besides, there is a great chasm separating us. No one can cross over to you from here, and no one can cross over to us from there.' ²⁷ "Then the rich man said, 'Please, Father Abraham, at least send him to my father's home.²⁸ For I have five brothers, and I want him to warn them so they don't end up in this place of torment.' ²⁹ "But Abraham said, 'Moses and the prophets have warned them. Your brothers can read what they wrote.'[30] "The rich man replied, 'No, Father Abraham! But if someone is sent to them from the dead, then they will repent of their sins and turn to God.' [31] "But Abraham said, 'If they won't listen to Moses and the prophets, they won't be persuaded even if someone rises from the dead.'" (TLB)

This parable is a lot more than a description of Hell being a hot place, but clearly in this parable Hell and the pre-location are HOT!! Notice how I use the term "pre-location." I do this because the Bible is very specific that when one dies that you don't go straight to Heaven or Hell. One thing we know from this parable is that Hell is for eternity not a period of time as taught by some. Matthew 25:41-46, Hebrews 6:2, and Jude 7 are quite clear. What does eternal actually mean? There are many verses that have Heaven as being eternal. Why would it not be possible to have an eternal punishment that goes along with an eternal trophy?

He was recognized by the spirits of Satan. The most obvious story is Matthew, Mark, and Luke.

Matt 8: 28-34 "When he arrived at the other side in the region of the Gadarenes, two demon-possessed men coming from the tombs met him. They were so violent that no one could pass that way. 'What do you want with us, Son of God?' they shouted. 'Have you come here to torture us before the appointed time?' Some distance from them a large herd of pigs was feeding. The demons begged Jesus, 'If you drive us out, send us into the herd of pigs.' He said to them, 'Go!' So they came out and went into the pigs, and the whole herd rushed down the steep bank into the lake and died in the water. Those tending the pigs ran off, went into the town and reported all this, including what had happened to the demon-possessed men. Then the whole town went out to meet Jesus. And when they saw him, they pleaded with him to leave their region." (TLB)

How do they know who he is? Why do they all refer to him as "the Son of God"? The Bible is chock full of numerous examples like this. This is just one example and there are several on this subject. James 2:19 states that demons "tremble with fear" at the knowledge of God. It seems that the Demons have more sense than most humans.

What about the "Hell on Earth" phrase? You already have read where I went through mine. As this book is being written, I have gone through five personal losses and all were very close to me. The saying is that he will not let you go through more than you can bear. I wonder sometimes what that level is? It seems to me that God has high expectations. I keep reminding myself that it could be worse. As bad as it is there has been worse. What about yours? Are you going through a rough time now or have been? To think there are people out there who believe that we are not in a spiritual battle on Earth even now.

So, is there a Hell? Are God and Jesus both liars? If they are, remember Revelation 21:8, basically stating liars will be fryers. Also, if there is no Hell, why would Jesus say this? What is the purpose of repentance? Without repentance, there is no need for the remission of sins. Why would Paul and others refer to a "race" and a crown in their letters? There is so much you have to ignore to have that kind of mindset. The way I see it, those that believe there is no Hell, have a lot of questions to answer. Remember, God does not change. There may have been a cross with his son attached to it involved, but God does not change. He is the same being in the New Testament and the Old Testament. For him to be called God. One of his characteristics is

IS THERE A HELL

he is Immutable. The way we approach or worship God is different, but God is the same yesterday, today and tomorrow. Did you know that there are more verses in the Bible describing Hell than there are describing Heaven? Yet, you believe in Heaven don't you? It seems to me that the shoe needs to be on the other foot. Those that believe there is no "Hell" need to explain their position instead of the other way around. My father always had a saying, "Without repentance there is no need for forgiveness." There are no accomplishments if there is no work involved in the final outcome. This flies in the face of all those that believe we all deserve a trophy.

This attitude of no "Hell" is a denial of what is taught by the Bible and a direct reflection of our society today. How is that you say? Let's look. Everyone gets a trophy these days. There is no "right" or "wrong" way to do something. Part of this is easily linked to the high rate of divorce in this country. All parents are trying to be "friends" with the kids. So it is a competition by the parents to get the kids whatever they want and there is very little or no physical discipline. I have seen this in my own family. It is such an accepted practice that it is everywhere you look and you are ridiculed if you do punish. There is even a joke in a movie. In it the kids are happy that Mom and Dad are getting a divorce. They say "yay!! Two Christmases"!! Although it is funny in the movie, we know in real life, it is the kids that pay the price. When I was in my youth, discipline was a common practice. My Mom had a practice of carrying a little red leather belt in her purse. We would go to the store and if we acted up the belt would come out and be placed like a necklace around her neck. It was rarely used, but there was an understanding of what it meant. Other times you would hear the statement, "don't make me take you to the car." Another thing would be an agreement that our parents had with the other parents in the neighborhood. If one of them saw us acting out or doing something that was inappropriate, then they could discipline us or call and tell our parents. You couldn't beat the speed of Ma Bell.

The favorite saying of all was "go to your room and wait till your father gets home". Going to your room didn't have the same meaning that it does today. There was not a tv or a computer in your room. Because of there only being one or two centrally located tvs, you

IS THERE A HELL

didn't have games in your room either. Only homework could be done to pass the time or your bed was available so you could take a nap. However, you didn't want to do anything. You had to anticipate the sound of the garage door opening and your father getting home and the corporal discipline that was to follow. One time I thought that I was being ingenious and asked if I could go to the restroom first. While there, I stuffed a couple of washcloths down my pants, thinking it would cushion the spanking that I was about to receive. It did cushion the blow. So much so, that it was quite obvious to the blow-giver. The answer was bare butt and an extra lick. Later in conversations with my father, I asked him if there was ever a time that he knew he shouldn't laugh, but did. He mentioned this incident and told me that after it was over he had to shut the door to his room so I wouldn't see how much he laughed afterward.

A few years ago, a co-worker and I were reminiscing about the discipline we received in our younger years. He grew up in the country where they have barns. He was one of six boys and could remember being taken on the other side of the barn to receive his corporal punishment. What is the saying, "take you out to the wood shed". The point being, you don't see this anymore. My co-worker and I talk about it as if it is times gone by. It is a time gone-by for us, as we are too old, but we talk about it because others around us don't receive discipline anymore. We have people that talk to us in a way that you wouldn't hear from us. If we had, we would have been "taken out to the wood shed" if we had talked to someone that way. Now it comes out what is stressful among the younger generations. One of the items on the list is losing wi-fi. Really?? This is what stresses you out? Yes, we do rely on the internet for almost everything. What will it hurt to pick-up a book to read. Maybe even the Bible. You see what I mean when we are a product of our society affecting the way we look at God.

Since we are on the subject of discipline, does God discipline? This goes along with our attitude here in society. If we shouldn't discipline our kids, neither does God punish people that have a faith in Jesus. So much so that now in our pulpits we hear nothing bad of God. In fact, they avoid the books of the Bible that have anything in it that might present God as anything, but love defined as society defines love today. Pulpits preach that "nothing but good comes from God" but when it is quoted in Romans 8:28 it is finished as "for those that love the Lord". In the case of the Israelite's, it was 400 years before God did amazing things. I wonder how many people plead with God during that time for the suffering to end? Things are on his time not ours. So we need to keep a check on reality when we look at the things of God and determine if the answer we give is the same one as quoted in the Bible.

Let's look at what the Bible says about discipline. We know the major things like the kicking out of the Garden of Eden when mankind made the decision to go against God. He even made sure that mankind was unable to get back in.(Gen.3:24,25) This was done by God, not Satan. Another obvious time of punishment is the Great Flood. Something about the flood, as far as we know, there was no rain prior to this time. In Genesis 2:6 some translations interpret it a mist or springs watered the earth. Imagine the surprise! God, that is God, killed all living beings on Earth. (Gen. 6) He, being God, made the Israelites wander through the desert for 40 years. How terrible! They had just come through so much. All because they rejected him. We also have Sodom and Gomorrah. (Gen 18:20-19:29) Cities soooo bad and taken over by evil that God had no choice but to destroy them. And in the one family that he had begged to save, the Mrs. died because she looked back and went against God's instructions. How dare we worship a God who is so harsh? That is the attitude that a large amount of the population would have today. Don't forget that the day of Jesus' death had an earthquake and a ghost infestation. (Matthew 27:45-52) They also had an eclipse, or something similar to it, for the first time recorded on the same day. Think of the self-restraint that was used by Jesus or God to not use the power that they had to stop the suffering and death. (Matthew 26:53)

Now let us look at something else. God told the Israelites to kill not just men, but women, children, and animals. This is detailed in Joshua 6. There are many studies out there that try to explain this order, but God ordered it and he had his reasons. There are cultures out there still that don't take prisoners and they have the same reasons. When you are asked to destroy a culture, then there is to be nothing left of that enemy. Anybody left will be an enemy to deal with down the road. You destroy a culture, so that they are not a problem down the road. It is hard for me, being an animal lover, to stomach this. We also have the story in the book of Judges chapter 7. In this story they are allowed to fight these people. And God determines the number of fighters, so that he can be glorified. There are numerous examples of how God is in charge of punishment in the Bible. So, again I quote:

> Romans 8:28 "And we know that God causes everything to work together for the good of those who love God and are called according to his purpose for them." (TLB)

Remember that God is immutable. To fit God into our standards is not only unacceptable, but without knowing the Old Testament, you don't know God. Have you ever noticed that the Psalms are picked through, so that only the Psalms about God's love are liked and all the other Psalms are discarded? Too many people think that if you know Matthew, Mark, Luke and John, then you know God. You may know part of the love of God and the fruition of his kingdom, but you will not know all of the true nature of God and his plan to be in relationship with man that he has had planned before the beginning. (I Peter 1:19 and Ephesians 3:9) How many miracles happen to us that we don't know or acknowledge? How many times has God protected you from something that you didn't know or talk about? You just knew and didn't tell anyone. How many un-explainable things have happened in your life? God is still very much active in our world. Why else would we pray and ask for certain things if God were not still active in our world?

Then there is Job. Job is a different character that we have to explain. Here is a man that had the kids and the "white picket fence." He had everything going for him that we can dream about. Then along comes Satan and he wants to test God. Basically, he made a bet with God. Satan bets God that Job will curse him if he strips him of his riches. That doesn't work, so Satan bets God Job's health. His friends even show up and tell him to curse God and be done with him. Ever have that happen to you? I did! My bad times don't even compare to Job's bad days. One of my friends literally sat me down and asked me "what have you done to God?" In the end, Job does not deny God and he is blessed with everything that Satan took from him plus some.

What do we take away from Job? First is that God has a "wall of protection" that God placed around Job where Satan couldn't touch him. He still protects us. How many times have you heard how people who were supposed to be on a flight that goes down and somehow miss the flight. You know those stories. How many times have you been late leaving for one reason or the other. Later you are stuck in traffic and you pass a wreck. Then you realize that if you had been on time, that could have been you. For me, I can remember a time when I was on a mountain climb. My hand slipped and I wasn't able to find another place to grip. When they say "your life will flash before your eyes", they are not joking. Not only does that happen in a dire situation, but time slows down. What seems like eternity is a split second. I had already looked for the closest tree and was going to jump. I figured it would hurt less and I had a better chance for survival if I jumped. The amazing thing was my hand was placed in a secure handhold and jumping was not necessary. You can say what you want, but for me it was God. There are other stories that I could share, but you see where I am going with this. God protects us. Sometimes it is very evident. Other times it is not so obvious.

God and Satan still interact. The book of Job presents Satan still coming into God's presence. Isn't it interesting that as bad as Satan is that he can still be in the presence of God. Kind of gives me some understanding of Salvation. No matter what I have done, I am still allowed into the presence of God. God asks me to be in his presence and discuss anything. Even the demons knew who Jesus was. Luke describes this in chapter 4 versus 40 and 41. Jesus had to shut them up because he wasn't ready for the people of the world to know who he was. Isn't it interesting that we work to be independent and live our lives on our own without God and deny him regularly. Yet, the demons knew who he was.

So, what does God want from us? For me, it is simple. He wants our hearts. You're either living for him or you're not. If there is no Hell, then it doesn't matter how one lives, you still get the prize. Yet the message is simple. Throughout the Bible the message is consistent, love God and love your neighbor. If you look at the

Ten Commandments, the first five commandments are about how to love God. The second part of the Ten Commandments are about how to love man. Then Jesus was asked what was the most important of all the Commandments. Matthew 22:34-40 tells about Jesus carrying on the theme of God first and man second. It is a consistent theme throughout scripture.

There are other examples in the Bible that need to be looked at as a guide for our lives. One is the Sermon on the Mount and the other is the fruits of the Spirit. Too many people consider any movement at all to be a work. However James chapter 2 talks about faith without works being dead. I look at it as side effects. One can debate whether the tree bearing fruit is referring to souls or Fruits of the Spirit, but either way, if you love Jesus, there will be side effects of people and Fruits based on that love. Some people think that being a tree that multiplies means how many people that you have converted in life. My question is "What if you live in a small town and everyone in that town is a believer. How do you multiply if your choices are limited by the number of people?" It just doesn't make sense and defies all logic. Then you have the school of thought that fruits are traits. This makes more sense to me. I figure that people see you living a certain way and some will chose to follow the Way.

The other thing that I look to is the Sermon On The Mount. This is a tough one because you don't know what to take literally and what to take figuratively. If we take it all literally, then you will find more people missing limbs than we do. If the Sermon On The Mount is taken figuratively, then some of the subjects that Jesus touches on are not applied that need to be put in our lives. Like I said, it is a tough one to read. Matthew chapters 5 – 7 are where the Sermon On The Mount is located. I rarely will tell you a book to read outside of the Bible, but when I do, then it helps with the study of the Bible. Unlike some today that use articles and books to live according to those items, the only book that needs to guide our lives is the Bible. Any outside books should help in our study of the Bible and not dictate our lives. With this said, one of the books that is recommended is "Sayings That Saved My Sanity" by James Woodruff. It is a book that includes the parables as well as the Sermon On The Mount. It brings these

IS THERE A HELL

items to life and does a good job of breaking them down into easy to understand stories. Jesus was a story teller. Today you can get a degree in story telling. It is an art. There is even a story telling festival that is held every year in a town here in Tennessee.

So what have we learned about Hell in the Bible? The Bible describes it. God and Jesus talk about it. The prophets talk about it. Followers of The Way talk about it. Hell is written about in both the Old and New Testaments. Hell is real folks!! There is an on going battle between good and evil. It doesn't matter that there was a cross. It only changed the way that we approach God. Even though Satan has been defeated, he is still trying to recruit numbers into his army. Remember, the power given to us by the comforter is eternal life. That doesn't mean we live forever in this world. It just means that we can be in God's presence throughout eternity with the power over death.

5
THE SEX STUFF

NOW WE COME to the part the book you may have skipped to. If you did, hopefully you will read the rest of the book. The marketing world says that "sex sells". While the general public pretends that it isn't affected. Guess what? Sex does sell!! However, that is not why this chapter is in this book. This subject is being addressed because "SEX" is a major issue that is prevalent today and has been throughout the ages. In my years, I have seen so many families and church groups torn apart because of views on this subject. We think that everyone that sits on those pews is to be perfect. We put on fake faces when we go to a worship place. In reality everyone that sits on those pews has a struggle of some kind. It makes me sick to see a set of parents reject a child because they are divorced and a second marriage (or more) is happening. Even though the couple is "shacking" up together, that is okay as long as marriage isn't brought up. This subject seems to be the biggest issue in people's lives. So let's unpack this bag and see what the Bible says about "sex".

The world tells us a lot about sex. To the world we should act like everything is normal to enjoy sex. What is it the movie tells us, by date 3 you should end it in

THE SEX STUFF

the bedroom. If you try to be good, the other partner then worries that something is wrong. Down the road they may tell you that they have no desire for anything. I know! You treat someone the way that they are supposed to be treated and you fail. How does the saying go? "Good guys finish last." There is some serious truth in that statement. I'm guessing that it applies to both sexes. You are damned if you do and damned if you don't. There is no winning. It is such a need that it has been added to Maslow's Hierarchy of Needs. If you are not familiar with this list, it is a basic list of needs that are needed in life, such as love, esteem, and safety. Now "sex" has been added to this list because it is such a desire. It is a basic need now. Now the world has changed its tactics and added more genders. In fact, now it is taught at schools that your sex isn't determined at birth. You get to decide as you get older. You see how the world progresses. First it is the issue of sex period. Next it is gender. If you don't agree with their tactics, you are a bigot, homophobe, etc. and people don't want to be called names, so they just clam up.

Religion acts like we are all goody-two-shoes and abstains from reality. In other words, it is one big lie, but it sounds good. When something happens (like a pregnancy), those that are in the Christian religion feign shock and appall. Leaving those that are the guilty parties feeling like there is no such thing as Grace and they are left feeling like victims of their actions. One thing that is a regular occurrence is preachers having affairs with someone that they are counseling. This happens, the elders announce the issue, then those that are involved lose their jobs as a church leader or are labeled. That person or persons then leave the group due to embarrassment. They then find another group that will accept them as is or leave religion all together thinking that there is no hope and their soul is forever doomed.

We have seen how the world and religion look at sex, but what does the Bible say. Not much is said about this act created by God. I say this because people tend to forget this fact. We picture Jesus as sexless. That is because it is not described in the Bible. We see what happens in religious groups that try to practice being sexless. The Bible does talk about marriage, but the subject of sex leaves a lot to be desired. It all starts in the book of Genesis chapter 2. God said it was not good for man to be alone. So he does surgery to man and makes woman from a rib. From then on, it has been work. No longer did man just tend a garden, but man and woman learned to live with each other. Or not. There is a lot about marriage in the Bible, but very little is mentioned in the Bible about sex. Marriage is so important in the Bible that it is used as an example between "the called out" and Jesus.

There are two categories of sexual sins. The first category is known as fornication. This is sex between a man and woman outside marriage. There is a print on my wall of the city during the Civil War. Outside the military camp is an area known as the fornication camp. This area is there for the guys in the military camp and it was a money maker for whomever set up the area. The second category is known as adultery. This is sex between a man and woman that aren't married. No matter what an individual thinks, loyalty is a huge thing in a relationship. You **will** be tempted sexually outside of marriage. It is usually the state of the relationships that leads to these temptations being acted on or not. There are other reasons, but each couple adopts whatever steps so that loyalty isn't an issue. This is one reason that the current Vice-president says that he will not eat alone with someone of the opposite sex without his wife being present. Some couples use the same email address. I know of companies that will not allow people of the opposite sex to travel together. They will book separate flights for these people. I also know companies that have it written in their manuals that if it is proven that you had an affair, the company will let you go. In other words, they will fire you. It is not to say that adultery is automatic in these situations, but there are steps that can be taken to keep loyalty at the forefront. We are all faced with fornication and adultery at some time in our lives, it is up to each couple to decide what actions to take to guarantee loyalty to the other partner.

This book is not meant to be a guide for long lasting relationships, but there are some things that I have seen over the years. One thing is sex. Don't base your relationship on sex. Relationships that develop fast rarely last long. As my father used to say, "what do you do when the heavy breathing ends." All relationships that last are based on the fact that the couple are friends. Friendship gets you through a lot of things up or down. How many of you call a friend when things go arry?

THE SEX STUFF

How nice it must be to have your spouse as a friend to help you get through the hard times and at the same time you want to spend time with them because you enjoy their company.

Another thing that I have noticed in lasting relationships is that they have common goals. How nice it is when you have two people that are both working for the same thing. No matter what comes up, if you have the same goal, it will be easier to get through. More times than I can count, I have seen it where one of the couple is in charge of the money. Either one or the other spouse doesn't like the other person to be totally in charge of how they spend money or one of the spouses is better at keeping the money under control or saving. I don't recommend that one spouse be over the money. The money thing is one of the top things that there is a fight about in married couples. If the couple works together on the money and has common goals, then arguments over money are severely curbed. However, maybe it works for you. If so, then so be it. Like I said, this book is not meant to be addressing relationships, it is just a couple of things that I have seen over the years.

The next subjects are probably controversial to you. The last thing I want to do is make the reader upset, but our society is such that some subjects need to be addressed. One thing to remember is that we live in a country that doesn't believe in God or Christianity as much. Maybe there are two things of which we need to be aware. The other thing is that sexual sins seem to be special sins. Is this a product of Christians? In the Bible, sin is all the same, but out here in the world it is not. I have had a person in my office that was accused of murdering their spouse. He was found not guilty, but that information didn't make the news. The damage was done. He was unable to keep his job. I had no choice, but to let him go. In this case, he was understanding. We were friends and I have been able to give him recommendations over the years. So don't believe what you are being fed. Check things out. Keep these things at the front of your mind as we look at the following topics.

The first subject has to do with how many genders are in this world. In our world today there is more than one gender. Are you aware it is even being taught in our schools? The teaching these days is that you are born as an "it" and you can decide what gender you

THE SEX STUFF

want to be as you get older. The main problem with this teaching is that it flies in the face of what is taught in the Bible. The first chapter of the book of Genesis is very explicit about the genders being made male and female. It doesn't say he made his creation as an "it." The book in the Bible is very explicit about what they were to do as well. I am fully aware that some of us are born as hemaphrodites. Just in case you are not sure about this word, it means people born with both sexual organs. It happens. However, there is a simple blood test done to determine a baby's sex. We are so being taught the exact opposite.

It is true that the Isrealites were commanded to have homosexuals put to death. This is still true today. If you live in a Muslim country, there is automatic death to those who practice homosexuality. This is why the press was in shock and disbelief when they interviewed a leader from a Muslim country and his response to someone asking about homosexuals in that country was "do you know of any?". Now the push in this country is for equal treatment. That is part of the reason it is labeled as a life style. Religion is also thrown in there because how can you be against homosexuality? This means you are judging and nobody wants to be labeled as a "judge." Even though right and wrong is all through out the Bible, to go with the Bible you must be a judge. Right? So sin is sin and should all be treated the same. Everyone has fallen short in one way or another. I hope that all Christians would want to help anyone because we all fight with something. The gathering of Christians is supposed to be a place of help for all people and to treat someone as different is not something I find. So should somebody that struggles with a sexual sin be allowed to serve others? Why not? We all struggle and need help on something. The problem comes in with those that don't believe that right and wrong are part of the Bible. This is where laws come from in a country. Can you imagine if you lived somewhere that had no driving laws and you could drive as fast as you wanted to drive? Look at what happens to church groups that still believe in right and wrong. Even the movies we watch and the news reporters on the television push a certain belief. Bad treatment comes on both sides of the argument. On one side you have certain people that consider sexual sins different. Then on the other side you have certain ones that get in your face and say, "I am a homosexual and you have to like it." Either way is wrong, but the media like a dispute and that is what makes news. Don't be drawn into a points war. Instead look to the Bible to answer your questions.

While sex has destroyed families and church groups, it is not mentioned as much as we would like in the Bible. You would think it would be mentioned more. There are so many things tied to it. If only it was talked about as much as marriage is mentioned. The topic of sex could be talked about more, but we will end this chapter with the story of the woman at the well. (John 4:1-42) There are many sermons here as well, but we are going to concentrate on what Jesus said to her. She had had five husbands and the man she was currently with wasn't her husband. How many people look to something else because they have been mistreated by their spouses or someone of the opposite sex? For me, it is cats. For others, it is something that shows they care. Maybe even this is what leads to homosexuality? Back to the story, she was told to go and sin no more. What was the sin he was specifically referring to? No matter what her sin, there was still hope for her. There is still hope for us as well.

6
DOWN TO THE RIVER

YOU LOOK AROUND and you see a church on every corner. There are many reasons for this or we just attend to belong to a group. We have never really studied and compared what is being taught or what is said in the Bible. This is especially true when we talk about salvation. Some groups believe that sprinkling is fine. Others think that the whole body gets dunked into water. And still others think that all that needs to be done is "call on the name of the Lord". So which is it? Are all these teachings correct? Are there multiple ways of salvation? Does it matter how old one is to be saved? These questions and others are ones that you should be asking. I would think that this is an important subject that one should study and is easily explained in the Bible.

We know what is out there. Let's look at what the Bible says about the subject of salvation. Another thing we need to remember is the entire Bible is a description of the relationship between God and mankind. Once again it starts with the Garden of Eden. Here mankind and God are in perfect relationship. He walks among them and talks to them. Everything is GREAT!! Then they do the one thing that God told them not to do.

They ate the fruit of the tree of Knowledge of Good and Evil. Now let's stop here. There are some people out there that say "it is the woman's fault" that man was brought down. Now I am as jaded as they come around, but even I don't fall for that argument. Man had seen that fruit on the tree and knew what it looked like. To say "he didn't know" is bogus. Everybody thinks that just because Eve was still standing and didn't die, that it must not be true. God knew something was wrong. Mankind "hiding" was a tell-tale sign that things had changed. What did die is the relationship between mankind and God. The rest of the Bible is God's effort to re-establish the relationship that was once there. To put it simply, you have the good relationship with God, the fall, God reintroducing himself to mankind, God coming to Earth, and how mankind and God can be in relationship again. One thing to remember is that God is immutable. He does not change. The only thing that changes is the way mankind approaches God. This is a very brief synopsis of the Bible.

The first thing we need to look at is the issue of sacrifice and blood. It all started when God was going to kill (yes, it was God doing this) all the firstborn males in

Egypt. This affected everyone. The only houses that the spirit by-passed were the houses that had blood spread on the doors. Can you imagine being there when the decree went out? You didn't have social media like you do today. So it had to be word of mouth. The presence of blood is very important. In this case, life or death are dependent on this. It is no different today if you think about it, it is a matter of life and death.

The high priest was the only person allowed to enter the Holy of Holies. To do this there were certain procedures that he had to go through to be in this room. (Leviticus 16) One thing he had to do was deal with blood and water. We know that on the cross that blood and water flowed from the body of Jesus. Apparently there is serious importance put on blood to be in the presence of God.

If I have not said it before, I will mention it now. God is immutable! He does not change. The only thing that changes is the way that we approach God. So how do approach God now? Too many people think that the blood shed on the cross covered all sins. We can behave however we want to. It doesn't matter because the cross covers all sins. Because of our attitudes today, the message in the Bible is being twisted to match our beliefs of the day. For instance, one of the common themes of the day is that everyone gets a trophy. Now you have people that cannot do any wrong. Do you see what I mean? These kids get out in the real world and it is not like this. No wonder these kids need their safe spaces. They have not been presented or faced with reality.

Now we are faced with the reality of our salvation. Does it seem fair that salvation applies to everyone no matter how they live? What do we do about those that lead good lives have the same reward as those that commit homicides? Since we categorize sins, let us mention these sins in the previous sentence. Have you ever noticed that all people are angels at their funeral? It wouldn't be profitable, either monetarily or numbers wise, if the life of the person is mentioned. Can you imagine if the person leading the funeral was honest about the person about whom they were talking? The more I write about this, the more questions come to mind. If you are a business owner, do you hire someone that doesn't have the same goals as you for the business? The same applies to God. Would you want someone around you that doesn't have the same vision as you? The question that is around today has to do with the payoff of student loans. The policy that is being debated is that the federal government will pay any loan you have to pay your tuition. The question is what about those who have sacrificed to build up accounts, so that the kids wouldn't have to have loans when they got to college? Do they get the money back that they have worked so hard for over the years? The answer from one of the candidates was "no." It is the same way with salvation. You do everything right, you have a giving heart, etc., why do those people get the same reward as those that don't? This is a modern day example that I am using in regards to salvation, but it also shows how the politics and attitudes of the day can affect how we worship.

We have seen how important it is in the Old Testament to touch the blood. So how do we touch the blood in the New Testament? It is interesting that baptism for forgiveness of sins started with Jesus. This practice continued in the book of Acts. In case you don't know, the book of Acts in the Bible is about the spread of Christianity. The baptism used in all examples is total immersion. Jesus also gave the commandment to go out into all the world and baptize people in certain names. Then we come to the example in Acts about the man in the chariot. What does he say? "What stops me from being baptized?" Why is this so important to him? Why is baptism mentioned so much in the book of Acts?

This brings up some other thoughts. Is baptism a sign or a necessity? There are church groups out there that have a baptism day. These are days where those that have decided to follow Jesus go through the motions of baptism. What happens to them between the time they have decided to be a Christian and baptism day? This is a group where baptism is a sign not a necessity. There are other examples, but this is one that comes to mind. I believe this argument is one that can go on till Jesus returns, by then it will not matter. However, when it comes to the examples, none of them have people waiting. When they hear the story of Jesus, they all participate in touching the blood right then. They don't wait.

We see it often. An announcement for a Christening or a baby baptism. Tell me something. Why are older people making the decision for someone younger, who can't even walk yet? Is this supposedly for any sins that they might commit during their life? One of the phrases you might hear used is "age of accountability." It is not found in the Bible, but it is frequently used. It refers to the age of a person when they are aware of their behavior. It can vary how old you are and you can argue that someone has never grown up, but it means that you are old enough to know that you want to commit your life to Christ. Notice that I used the word "commit" in the previous sentence. That is because God wants our hearts. He has done so much for us. Even gave his son to death. Why would he not want the same dedication from us? The point is that in all of the examples of baptism, it is always an older person who chooses to participate in the act. You will be hard pressed to find an example in the Bible where someone is not old enough to understand the decision they have made.

There is one other thing we need to mention. There are doubts in our minds that God would not be so ritualistic. Especially about something that happened at the cross with the death of his son. I get it. It is symbolism over substance. However, we have to look at one thing.

He instituted the Lord's Supper. Jesus did two things in his ministry. He did the Lord's Supper for one and the second thing that he did was baptism.

Something that is apparent about salvation is that it seems to be a matter of attitude. If one desires to be a part of Christianity, he will participate in all the actions. The "side effects" will be evident in their lives. Another thing we have to notice is that somehow and at what point do we touch the blood. Blood is necessary in our salvation. Did God apply the blood to the door posts himself or did those in the house have to do it themselves? We had a saying in construction that the job is never complete without a blood sacrifice. This applied to someone that had smashed a finger or cut themselves somehow during the job. I have heard all the arguments like the traveling before your baptized, death bed confessions, the thief on the cross and others. I revert back to the fact that it is an attitude. I can't get past the examples in the Bible. All that I know is that he doesn't describe judgment for nothing. This is not meant to be a "Hell fire" book, but at some time we have to look at what we are being taught by those in whom we trust. Why is there a church on every corner? Are you attending worship services because it is where your parents went, are you attending somewhere to belong, they have the biggest building in the area, they have the nicest organ, etc.? The main reason to associate with others is because you all seek after the truth.

7
THE STUFF NOT TALKED ABOUT

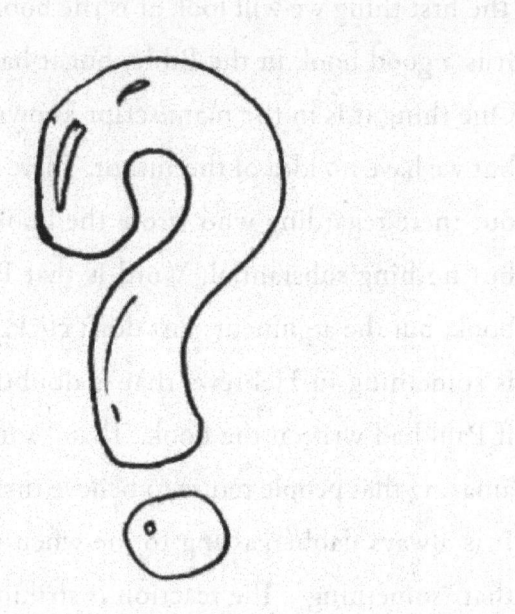

WELL NOW WE come to the chapter that will bring a lot of reaction. You will either throw this book away and chalk it up to wasted money, attribute the teachings to someone who is lost in his way, or you will get your Bible out and actually study it. No matter which option you choose, this chapter is going to make you sit up and think.

The first thing that we will mention is Inspiration. We have heard that the term means "God breathed" and that it applies to the whole Bible. However, things are not quite right when we get down to the brass tacks. The first thing we will look at is the book of Hebrews. It is a good book in the Bible, but it has some issues. One thing it is in the manuscript known as the Bible, but we have no idea of the author. There are arguments out there regarding who wrote the book of Hebrews, but nothing substantial. Word is that Paul wrote the book, but the arguments just don't click. Besides, there is something in Hebrews that is doubtful to happen if Paul had written the book. That " something" is so amazing that people refuse to believe that it is possible. It is always flabbergasting to me when you point out that "something". The reaction is striking to me, even by those who are supposed to be scholars, pretend that they never knew, or they knew and it was ignored. That "something" is that there is an error in the book of Hebrews (Heb 9:3,4). There! I said it. I can hear the sound of this book hitting the floor as people throw it away. Maybe some of you will pick up your Bibles and look and see that what I am telling you is true. It is a simple mistake, but it is there none-the-less. In the temple you had two rooms, the Holy Place and the Most Holy Place. The Most Holy Place was reserved for one piece of furniture. That was the Ark of the Covenant. All the other furniture was to be kept in the Holy Place. This included the Altar of Incense (Exodus 36). Yet, in Hebrews, the Altar of Incense is listed in the Most Holy Place. If not an error, than a serious oversight. But that would be a justification of the error. We do that for all sins as well. We justify all sin when we are faced with temptation. Just a little side note. Some of you will try and explain this error. It is only natural to defend the things that are personal to us.

The second part about inspiration are the books of the Bible, Luke and Acts. (Luke 1:1 – 3) Luke specifically mentions that what he wrote was investigated.

That alone should bring a question to the readers brain. Why would you need to investigate if you are inspired by God? In fact, there are times that he is not present with Paul in the book of Acts. You can tell this by the language used. Not to say there is anything wrong with these books being investigated, as long as what is presented is truth. The presentation of truth used to be something that the press was guilty of in this country, but that is another issue for another chapter. The point here is that inspiration is not the definition that we have believed or been given all our lives.

We need to spend time talking about sibling rivalries. It is something that happened in the beginning to now. We still have issues between brothers and sisters even today. We all know about Cain and Abel. They were brothers and one was jealous of the other. This led to one committing murder. This is the first recorded murder. There are other sibling rivalries mentioned in the Bible. We also know of Isaac and Esau. (Gen 25) In this example, we know that Isaac was a twin brother. He was born holding the ankle of his brother, Esau. Later in life, Esau sold his birthright to his brother for a bowl of soup. Now for another question. Did God carry out his mission with whomever was the firstborn or did he already have it planned who would do his bidding? Today we still have the firstborn, but do they get any special treatment? I can tell you that those that are firstborns DO expect certain things. They do get treated differently by the parents. For awhile, I used to work in the x-ray department in a hospital. The x-ray tech and I used to play a game of guessing what order of birth the child was based on how they were treated by the parent. The same thing happened with Abraham and Sarah. They were promised that their lineage would be passed on like sand on the beach. In other words, IMMESUREABLE. They were unable to wait on God so Sarah told her handmaiden (servant) to have a sexual relationship with her husband and give him a son. The sermons here are numerous, but that isn't the purpose here. Ever wonder what happened to the descendants of that son? Did the promises from God carry over to all descendants of Abraham? You don't want to know what I think. Just read the text and make your own decisions. Did the promise from God eventually lead to another religion? It would be interesting if this sibling rivalry is what eventually leads to the war we know as

Armageddon. The point here is to notice how sibling rivalries play a huge part in our history. They are still a part of families.

Now we come to a topic that none of us want to believe. It goes against everything we have been taught and believed because we trusted the people that did the teaching. However, this subject is in the Bible and we need to address it. The topic is predestination. How many of us believe that there is no way that God would circumvent the saving or condemnation of someone? We all have freedom of choice. Right? Yet, we have examples of God acting through certain people to accomplish his will. Do you think Moses just happened to be in the area when the burning bush incident happened? After all, he was a murderer. Before that, you have the story of Jacob and how he saved the known world at the time, but especially the people that God would later save. Let's move to the New Testament and check out some examples there. Jesus even talked about his death (Luke 9: 22 – 24). Jesus even knew how he was to die. Have you heard of Jonah? Here is a man that tried to go against God and we see what happened to him. Do you think he had a choice? Why would God not pick someone that was not more confidant instead of going to all that trouble? It didn't stop there. Lets talk about Paul. Here is a man that God chose to carry his teachings all over the world (Acts 9:15). No wonder he was able to survive all those shipwrecks and being bitten by a snake. It still continues today. Did you know that George Washington was shot four times and never got hit? He even got to the point he was beginning to believe that he was invincible. Another fairly modern-day example is General George Patton. From WWII, he is a man that believed in predestination. Even in the movie they mentioned this. He believed he was born to win wars. He was able to "smell" a battlefield. Everyone that served under him will tell you that he did not stop. So now we have to ask ourselves this question. Are we meant to carry God's mission for one reason or another?

How many of you love Christmas? I love the atmosphere of the season, the decorations, the food, and the music. I hate the day it is time to take down the decorations. This could be for the fact that the house looks drab or it might be because I want to share my house with friends and family. Do I have family to spend time with? Not really. I fully understand why this time of year is so hard for some people. Most importantly is the time off from work for most people. However, we need to talk about this one thing because so many people believe this. Another reason I hate to bring this up is because there is a war going on against Christmas. The thing we need to bring up is that it is not the birth of Christ. This holiday was put in place to cover up a celebration the Gentiles had. Have you ever wondered why it is not the same day in other countries? The reason for this is so the different groups can lay claim on what day this event occurred. We also know from the event described in the gospels that the shepherds were attending to their flocks. This didn't happen during the winter when the holiday occurs. Don't get me wrong. I have no problem observing the fact that God came to Earth in human form. Unfortunately, the search for truth is not the reason we have a war going on. Instead the people against Christmas don't like it because they don't like God at all. Probably because they are against anything with standards. They are having an effect as well. Not much right and wrong these days is there?

THE STUFF NOT TALKED ABOUT

We started with his birth, now we need to talk about his death. It makes for a good day off, but we need to look at this subject. How many of you think that sabbath means "seven?" I would guess it to say that many of you do. The word actually means "rest" and we have the problem of "special sabbath" mentioned in the Bible. Did the Jews use this word as we use the word "holiday" to mean a day off?

Another thing about his death is when did the last supper occur? We have been told for years that the meal Jesus had with his disciples is the Passover meal. However, in all accounts it might have been the preparation for the Passover Meal. If that is the case, then the bread that they ate was made with yeast. Yeast is representative of sin throughout the Bible. Jesus mentioned several times that he was the Passover lamb. Is it possible that he meant this literally? After all, Jesus did say he was taking on the sins of the world.

How many times in Jesus' life did he refer to himself as "the Passover lamb?" Was the title that he gave himself a literal one or was it figurative? These are legitimate questions that need to be asked about this subject.

There is more that we could mention, but to keep this chapter short, we will only mention briefly the dates. We still live today under the Gregorian calendar. The Israelite day was dusk to dusk. Based on this information, you can follow the calendar and the days just don't make since. Therefore, I will hold to Jesus being crucified on a Thursday. Not Friday as we are all led to believe.

I know that most people will not hold to these beliefs. There are too many people with a lots of initials after their last names that believe differently. One thing I can say based on the things that are mentioned in the Bible, a lot of people will be reading their Bible. There was a time that I thought I was alone in these beliefs. Then I found others. If I can say one thing, it would be, pick up your Bible and read. You might find it interesting and leaving you with several questions.

8
THE POLITICAL CHAPTER

HERE IS THE political chapter that I promised was coming. Politics is like death and taxes, you cannot avoid it. It is everywhere you go. From your place of work to family, to, yes, even your church family. Where I used to worship, used to be a place one could go to get healing. Then one day it started. Someone got up to lead that prayer. In that prayer, he mentioned the DACA kids. On top of that, the preacher later said we had a duty to cross the aisle with groups that believed in lies. That was enough for me, and I left that church group. Even our weather and science have become political and the more initials they have after their names, the smarter they must be. Sadly to say, it is even in us. To say that one is not influenced by politics is a statement of ignorance. It is hard to get the family together for the holidays without something being mentioned. God forbid you voice a differing opinion. You either agree or you are rejected. You are given the blame for "turning over the apple cart". In a sense, we are already in a civil war. Some on both sides have taken up arms. Don't think that Las Vegas wasn't a cover-up. I have seen them before and that one was botched. It scares me. One time I was told by a guy who used to work for an American intelligence agency that if the public knew what we stopped on a regular basis, we would be afraid to leave our homes. Too many times have I seen where there is no discussion of a subject, only raw emotion. Even Jesus had to deal with the politics of the day. Matthew 17 tells the story of the fish and the coin. Jesus is quite frustrated with the leaders because he is being forced to pay a tax for entering a place to worship. Jesus tells Peter to cast his net and the fish that is caught will have a coin in its mouth. It is the exact amount needed for both of them to enter. Could Jesus have made a big to-do about it? Sure! Did he? No! Maybe it was the timing thing again.

Now to tell you a story. I have been to Russia. (There's that collusion thing again) This trip included Moscow and a town called "Vorkuta". It is here we made friends with the town mayor, presenting him with a gift and a letter from our hometown mayor. The town of Vorkuta is located above the Arctic Circle. That was a first for me. At the time of year I was there, it was daylight for 24 hours. There literally is no darkness. Talk about messing with your internal clock. Finally, you just sleep from pure exhaustion. It is here that I learned how small the world really is. A team of people followed us. One guy showed up early due to his schedule. He and I were up one night (day) discussing things. In the course of our discussions, he described his house and parents. When I was in college, I was in a traveling group. Those of us in the group stayed in people's homes. Come to find out, I had stayed in his house and met his parents. Here we were halfway around the world and I find out that I had been in his home and met his parents. Talk about a small world.

Another lesson that I got from that trip was I got to mingle with the general population. Believe it or not, they speak better English then most people in this country. One of the topics that came up was what we are taught in school. I was there right after the fall of Communism, what was known back then as Glasnost. These people were learning how to live in the new society. To fill the void, the Russian Mob took over. The people didn't know how to live. All of the people had steel doors because they did not dare keep their money in the banks. If the businesses or banks didn't pay the "protection" money, they ran the chance of being burned out. There were a lot of burned out places.

THE POLITICAL CHAPTER

Most important was the one thing they mentioned and that was they were not taught that the U.S.A. was an enemy. It was a shock to me. We had also been told that there were bread lines. The stores didn't have the refrigeration that we have here. Therefore there were lines to get fresh produce on the days that shipments came in. Don't get me wrong. There are plenty of bad things that come from living under a communist dictatorship. I'm only saying that everything is not quite what is being told. This was to be my last trip across the "pond". When they announced that we were in American airspace, everyone clapped. This is a regular occurrence, because everyone realizes what it is like in their home countries and are thankful to be in America.

It hasn't changed today. In fact, it has progressed. In case you have not put two and two together, I am talking about your media. It has become a tool that spreads un-truths like it is the story of the day. It was a monopoly during my college DJ days and it continues today. Before you read your news from a ticker-tape generated by one group. You had no idea if what you were presenting as news was true or not. You assumed that the news that is being presented to you is the truth.

While the technology has changed, the news is still gotten in the same manner. Do you see how the same thing applies to the things you believe? It is presented as truth and the general public soaks it up as truth without confirming what they are being told. DO NOT BELEIVE WHAT YOU ARE BEING TOLD EITHER FROM THE SCREEN OR PULPIT. Even those with good intentions may have gotten their information from a bad source.

What is happening today is worse than any Communist country I have been in. Not only are you being given bad news, but your news is also being dictated by the likes and the dislikes of those who determine what to tell and how to tell something. The Press in Communist countries are controlled by those who rule. Here, it is determined by those that own and the upper echelons. Now it is a monopoly that is controlled by a group of individuals who determine what will be the news of the day. This wasn't noticeable when the religion was similar in this country. Now that the world has taken over, look out! You are being influenced every day. In fact, you still listen to the music, watch the tv shows, or movies as if it is normal. Even if what is contained within these media is contrary to what the Bible says. Your religious beliefs are being questioned if they haven't already been swayed one way or the other. People don't believe what is wrong anymore is a bad thing. Grace has taken over and turned the wrong into acceptable. Just like people don't know what is really happening in the world, so too, they don't know the Bible. The information contained in this book is a shock and most, if not all, will be written off.

Have you heard? The world is ending soon! According to some our planet will soon be uninhabitable. It is so much of a fear that young folks literally think that is true. That is why getting to Mars is such a big thing these days. Being one that has reached half a century in life, I do not fear this event happening as much as younger folks. However, what does the Bible say about the end of the world? In the book of Genesis, you have the story of how God was disappointed with his creation and punished it by destroying the Earth by sending the great Flood. All people descended from Noah and his family. Isn't it likely that the story of the flood would be passed down through the generations of all people? This was such a big deal. Remember, rain had not been recorded before this time.

God made a promise after the flood. That promise stated that he would no longer destroy the Earth by water. Genesis 9:1-17. Then Paul describes in his letter to Peter that it will be fire that destroys the Earth. More than that these verses also describe the end to be like a thief in the night. (II Peter 3:10) We don't know when a thief is going to break in to our home. If we knew, then we would take measures to keep that from happening. Jesus goes on to describe this in Matthew 24:36. Not even he knows the time when he is coming back to Earth. Yet people keep trying to predict the end of the Earth. Those who do either don't know their Bible very well or have an ulterior motive in mind.

This, of course leads in to the next big headline of the day. That would be the headline of climate change. I have lived long enough to see several destructions of the world happen. Just before I was born, we were afraid of the nuclear holocaust. That never happened except the Bay Of Pigs was awfully close. When I was born, we had the "energy crisis". Supposedly we didn't have energy to last us very long. So a lot of people had small families or no children at all to combat the "energy crisis". Any true physics teacher will tell you "there is no such thing as an energy crisis". Energy exists all around us. We have lived through the "ozone hole crisis". One of the things out of this is the refrigerant we use today to charge up our A/Cs. Now we have left "Global Warming" and evolved into "climate change". Why is there a group of people that want mankind to live in tepees? It is more proof that science is politicized. No one is saying that mankind doesn't have a responsibility to be honorable with what it discharges. However, the thought that mankind can destroy the world that God created is absurd. One thing you can always do is follow the money. I have seen how investors protect themselves. The only ones that get caught are the ones who have made somebody mad.

The other big headline of the day is "collusion". Everybody believes not only did Russia steal the election, but they were able to infiltrate the actual voting machines and turn the election. We now know this to be untrue, but it is a very good example. Not only is what in the news a lie, also what you believe about the

Bible may not be what it seems. However, there was collusion! The more I hear and the more evidence that is learned, there is no way that our current President should have won. We know that God has direct influence on things in this world to accomplish his plans for this world. Is it beyond imagination that God put a man like Trump in charge of this country? The pigs are squealing as well. I use that phrase because Jesus was recognized by the demons and they begged him to cast them out to the swine. The pigs then ran off a cliff. That is what I refer to when I use that phrase. The current President is interrupting money both countrywide and worldwide. Before, there was a group of people that tried to move toward the world being under one rule. It is what is known as "Globalism." However, people who believe that don't know their Bible very well or they would remember the story of Babel. More than that, they only have power and greed in their thoughts and actions.

The next topic is one that has been discussed since the Supreme Court case of Roe vs Wade. That's right!! It is time to throw in abortion here. It is the big discussion lately because of the fear by the World of that decision being overthrown. It is only a matter of time before that incident occurs. Don't think the pigs won't squeal the closer that day approaches and afterward. Being someone that studied pre-med in college you study the techniques and practices that are used in this procedure. No matter what trimester it is, the procedure is butchery. Abortion leads to higher levels of depression and guilt. First, you are depressed for the life that is no longer in you and you feel guilty about the action itself. Now I am in no ways judging. I have had my fair share of issues that I thought kept me from God. However, when you have cheering for abortion laws passed and when you have a state Governor making a statement about what is tantamount to infanticide, you have a problem. On top of that, you see how the attitude about sex has led to this. One issue leads to another. The problem is the "World" creeping in to the way of thinking.

Immigration, that is a touchy subject. Now here is an issue that effects even the staunchest of Bible thumpers out there. I have heard and read the propaganda that is out there on this issue. My favorite thing to hear is that we are all migrants. Weeellll!! Is this statement true or false? Notice how religion is thrown into the argument when they say "Jesus was an immigrant". Both of these statements are false, but if you aren't prepared, you might think these statements sound pretty convincing.

First off, most of you are not immigrants. There is a definition of an immigrant. Those that profess the teaching that "you are an immigrant" are trying to change the definition of the word and what you think. Most of you are born into the countries where you live. America was not yet a country at the time of it's infancy. Therefore, there were no laws in place at the time. But you say, what about those that already lived here? Did the Isrealites complain about the countries they conquered and people that they were commanded by God to kill just so they can have a land of their own?

Secondly, Jesus was an immigrant for a period of time. That part is true. To avoid being put to death, his parents took him to Egypt. We are not told what the immigration laws are for Egypt at the time. Were Jesus and his parents illegal? That seems to be most of the problem. Most people are not making a distinction between legal immigrants and illegal immigrants.

THE POLITICAL CHAPTER

No matter what a person is, he is to be treated as a neighbor. The laws of the land are determined by those in charge. However, the Bible is very specific about how to spread the news about go and teach. Too many times people think that bringing people here, will allow them to be taught Christ or the American way. Unfortunately, immigrants come here and get into their clicks of others from their countries. This allows them to maintain their cultures that they are used to in a new land. God gave very specific commands on how to keep the lands pure. I remember, in college, how people that enrolled had to go through an orientation. Here they were taught how to do laundry and most of all how Americans shower everyday. Believe it or not, it is not normal to shower every day like we do. How we live is a cultural thing and we must help others that want to learn the American culture.

By the way, this leads me to mention one thing. The United States of America is the greatest country in the history of the world. Just had to say that!! It is true!! No other country in the world is like this country. There is no wonder that people want to come here in droves. The one color they see, that we all need to see, is green.

The amount of wealth that is available in this country far surpasses any other country. That is why you have to take precautions when in foreign lands. Is there any doubt this country is blessed by God?

This section is going to make some readers upset. Your emotional reaction only furthers my argument that the World is totally entrenched one way or another in your religion. This section is referring to these groups that spring up based on lies. Like all groups that develop, it is seen as a good thing, but still stems from a lie. It really chafes me to hear someone tell me that I need to "cross the aisle". Some things are meant to be negotiated. Other things are not meant to be negotiated. The biggest thing that chafes me is when people inject their political stances into the worship. Have you ever heard someone lead the worshipers in prayer and pray about something that is illegal, based on the laws of the day? Have you ever heard a preacher throw politics into the sermon?

When we talk about groups, we will talk about a couple of groups that are prominent today. We will start with the #metoo movement. So many people believe it is a movement based on something good.

However, if you do a deep dive into the issue, you see that it has its flaws. Unfortunately, there are bad things that happen based on the sex of a person, but it goes both ways. Also, you have the leader being arrested for having a "boy" of which she took advantage. It makes me want to start the #menow group. The hypocrisy is written all over this movement. It lumps all men into the category of being "bad". Have you noticed how all men portrayed in shows on television are "stupid"? How many men are confused because the roles in the family are not clearly defined? Come to think of it, do you see how the world is destroying the family? There are no more roles anymore. You say, "it is easy for me to say, you are a guy and jaded at that." I am just telling what I see. Maybe this is another influencer of the high divorce rate in this country. Earlier I told you that I worked in a locked psych unit. Many people that were admitted with depression were being afflicted by the spouse. I saw it both ways. This movement started based on a lie and has spread to all sections of our society. It is a movement that has affected the way we treat those of the female sex. Don't think this movement doesn't affect your religion.

Another movement we will mention is Black Lives Matter or BLM for short. This group started as an off shoot of the incident where a guy was shot by a cop. All the sayings by the media and others over the groups said what happened was he held up his hands and yelled "hands up, don't shoot". The truth doesn't fit the narrative. However, the investigations explain something else happening. According to the investigations, he reached in to the car and tried to steal the gun away from the cop. This is not to say that a black man isn't shot by a white cop. Even though the numbers indicate that it happens rarely. Does it happen? Sure it does. How many of you people that are reading this book, have rejected someone because of skin color yet claim to be religious. How many of you will believe what is said about me just because I wrote this book? You can start groups to make yourself a victim if you want, but this is a bad example and based on a lie.

Don't get me started on the group called Antifa. It is nothing more than the modern day version of the KKK. You might be surprised who is in this group if they didn't wear those masks.

THE POLITICAL CHAPTER

Something else we need to mention is "equality". We are beaten with this subject all the time. We are made to believe that all people are on the same playing field. Instead of bringing up all people to a higher plane, we have dumbed down our society to make us equal on a lower playing field. There is not equality in Heaven. Even the angels have a hierarchy. The Seraphim and Cherubim are just to name some. We don't know how to achieve rank. However, maybe it is something as cliché as "every time you here a bell, an angel gets its wings". The opportunity for salvation is the same in the Bible for everyone. Kind of like the opportunities that are available in this country. However, because of certain backgrounds or other reason, some of us stay stuck. Some break the mold. Listen to what God is telling you.

Like I said earlier, "to say that you aren't political is a statement of ignorance". I guarantee you that you have an opinion about one or more of these subjects. Not only will you have an opinion about these issues, but you will judge a person based on the way another person feels about the subjects. I have noticed over the years, that the closer one is or if you live in a blue county, Grace rules supreme and allows you can do almost anything. Whereas, if you're in red district, it is more judgmental. There is a fine line between grace and judgment.

9
THE SUM OF ALL THINGS

That's the whole story. Here now is
my final conclusion: Fear God and obey
his commands, for this is everyone's duty.
God will judge us for everything we do,
including every secret thing,
whether good or bad.

Ecclesiastes 12: 13, 14

SO HOW DOES this book end? With the Grace of God. That is how it ends. God is involved in this world and what occurs within it. Those that were "followers of the Way" in the early days had the Septuagint and still taught salvation. Today we have multiple translations available to us. Each has its good points and bad points. Yet we can still teach Salvation. How do we live? Remember that the best sermon taught is the one that is lived, not the one that you hear spoken from a pulpit or read.

After all the teachings that are out there by organized religion and the world, how do we know we have the correct books? With all the untruths coming out of pulpits, is there any hope? Hopefully you have not seen this book as a "Hell, fire, and brimstone" book. There is a balance, when the verse says "fear", I believe it is a respect. Fire can do a lot of bad damage if it is not controlled. We use fire for a lot of things and respect it. As long as we respect fire, we get a bunch of enjoyment out of it. It is the same way with God for me. God loves us so much, but he needs to be respected. God has done his part, he is calling mankind to do his part. Time and time again, he knocks. The purpose of this book is to slim things down from the thousands of pages of Bible studies that are out there and the pulpits that are at every corner. This book is not meant to scare you, but to make you want to grab your Bible or buy one and get to reading. The chapters have addressed how it all began, some of the major topics of the Bible, and topics that are not usually discussed in the Bible. It is not up to anyone to define the morality as God describes in the Bible. Yet, if you watch the media, they define right and wrong. They interview and rejoice with religious groups that pit one group against the other and praise groups that make wrong, right. We need to remember the woes in the Bible. Especially the one that talks about making the good evil and evil good. (Isaiah 5:20)

Let's end with a story. Suppose we go against what the Bible teaches and know when the end of the earth is going to happen. Let's use the example of a comet hurtling towards earth. We know that the earth is to be destroyed by fire. We just don't know when. The comet is scientifically studied. We know the when, we know the where, and we know the how. Are you focused on the condition of your soul during your last days or are you focused on your family? Do you face the impending doom with bravery or is there total trepidation? Are you running trying to survive as long as you can? At the last minute, the impending comet is stopped. Life goes on and there are celebrations everywhere.

We have this scenario in our Salvation. We were doomed and then we were saved.

I once read an article that I think perfectly describes what I think that Jesus meant the church to be:

> What if the church were not a building or meeting time? Not a "power bloc" vying for influence within the world's political structures? Not a self-serving institution whose central goal is maintenance of property, status, and budgets? What if the church were a microcosm of the kingdom of God that focuses the great variety of personalities, gifts, and passions of people to the single task of honoring God in the world? With different groups of Christians seeing the good in one another? With all of them looking for ways to serve and honor the non-Christians around them? What if the church were to embrace a lifestyle of humility and obedience, faith and

love, integrity and virtue—concerned more to be the Living Body of Christ than to own property or hold big rallies or sway the outcome of political contests? The church is supposed to be a pilgrim community of people so deeply committed to Christ that we are collectively a "third race of humanity"—beyond the customary biblical categories of Jew and Gentile—in which God can put on display the life he originally intended everyone to experience. It stands as a witness to the larger culture about what is possible for those who have not yet repented of their self-directed lives in order to believe the good news that God's kingdom rule is yet possible. Jesus instructed: "Go out and train everyone you meet, far and near, in this way of life, marking them by baptism in the threefold name: Father, Son, and Holy Spirit. Then instruct them in the practice of all I have commanded you. I'll be with you as you do this, day after day, right up to the end of the age" (Matt 28:19-20 MSG). The church is not buildings and property. It is not religious assemblies and ceremonies. It is not alignment with certain social causes or political parties. The church is a community of redeemed people in process of daily surrender to God's rule. The church is—in the version of Matthew just quoted—a distinctive "way of life" being modeled by already-Christians to not-yet-Christians. With the imprint left by Constantine beginning in the fourth century, this vision for the church faded. The church lost its calling to be a microcosm of the kingdom reign of God for the sake of becoming a location, an event to witness, a political force, or an entity whose favor could be courted by the world. Over time, a theology emerged that absolutized church over kingdom, prioritized church membership over Spirit-transformed lives, and changed corporate worship from participation to passivity. Along the way in Christian history, Christians became consumers, and churches competed with one another to sell their theology, their worship, and their ability to meet felt needs. Christians belong in the marketplace of ideas to be what Martin Luther dubbed "a sort of Christ" there. But we have turned churches into Christian ghettos and isolated ourselves from the world. We have put our hope in Sunday morning worship in church-owned properties rather than in the power of the Holy Spirit to disperse us into all the places we go to demonstrate that the One in us is greater than the Evil One who is prince of this world. We need to implement an authentic priesthood of all believers. Go into our offices, homes, classrooms, and workplaces as Christ's servants. Go there in the humility of the Son of Man. Offer no judgments or directives; be confessional about our own inadequacies and modest about our accomplishments. We should not ask to speak; we should be Christ's presence so authentically that we will be asked to explain ourselves. Then we bear gentle, faithful witness to the one who is our Lord. Such persons would be called anything but self-righteous hypocrites. In their reverent use of the name of Jesus, they would receive a more respectful hearing than is the case in so many venues where the Church of Sanctified Religiosity intrudes today. If the claim that the earliest church was "turning the world upside down" was true in its time (see Acts 17:6), it certainly is *not* true today. The church is often viewed as nothing more than an irritating irrelevance by our world. So perhaps it is the church that needs to be turned upside down—divesting itself of the pagan style of leadership that puts the powerful few at the top and embracing the Jesus style of leadership that understands serving as leading and humility as greatness. May it be so in our time—and until Christ comes. Only then may we be said to be praying with authenticity the words of the Lord's Prayer: "Your kingdom come, your will be done on earth as it is in heaven." By Rubel Shelley

The Grace of God is a beautiful gift. One that we should all strive for in this world. However, the relationship with God is a two-way street. Faith is our part that is forgotten by so many. The Office of the Vice President is being harassed for their faith, are you being harassed for your faith? Several of us put the status of our souls in other people's hands. It is such an important subject (eternity) that I would think that more people would want to check out what they are being told. It is like having a guarantee for something and you don't know the details of what is covered. Don't be one of those people that dislike a subject or a person and haven't even heard personally what is stated or the person that made the statement. You base your judgment on what is said about a statement or person. For instance, you may hear something about this book or me and haven't even read the book at all or in its entirety. How many times have I heard people say that they don't like a certain person because of what they hear that the person has said that has been totally taken out of context? Another saying that I have heard is "how can you just say something like that." Even though there are facts to back up the statements, if it is different from what they already believe, they object to the statement. Another saying that I have heard over the years is "I can't worship a God that does such things". Spoken by those that have been brought up listening to the world and letting it influence what they believe. Hopefully this book has opened the eyes of some and they will endeavor to read the Bible.

Remember the simplicity of the Bible. You have mankind and God living in harmony, Garden of Eden. Then you have the Fall of mankind from God, kicked out of the garden. The rest of the Bible is about God restoring his relationship with mankind. Pick it up and read it. Stop letting pulpits and those around determine your morals in life. Yeah, the genealogies can get boring, but there is everything else in there to capture your attention. There is politics, murder, intrigue, and religion of all kinds. There are many folks that sit through a movie that depicts certain things as porn that also sit in the pews each Sunday. Imagine if the interest was the same for the books of the Bible.

This book will end with the same words Paul used when his life was ending.

> **1** I solemnly urge you in the presence of God and Christ Jesus, who will someday judge the living and the dead when he comes to set up his Kingdom. ² Preach the word of God. Be prepared, whether the time is favorable or not.

Patiently correct, rebuke, and encourage your people with good teaching. [3] For a time is coming when people will no longer listen to sound and wholesome teaching. They will follow their own desires and will look for teachers who will tell them whatever their itching ears want to hear. [4] They will reject the truth and chase after myths. [5] But you should keep a clear mind in every situation. Don't be afraid of suffering for the Lord. Work at telling others the Good News, and fully carry out the ministry God has given you. [6] As for me, my life has already been poured out as an offering to God. The time of my death is near. [7] I have fought the good fight, I have finished the race, and I have remained faithful. [8] And now the prize awaits me—the crown of righteousness, which the Lord, the righteous Judge, will give me on the day of his return. And the prize is not just for me but for all who eagerly look forward to his appearing. [9] Timothy, please come as soon as you can. [10] Demas has deserted me because he loves the things of this life and has gone to Thessalonica. Crescens has gone to Galatia, and Titus has gone to Dalmatia. [11] Only Luke is with me. Bring Mark with you when you come, for he will be helpful to me in my ministry. [12] I sent Tychicus to Ephesus. [13] When you come, be sure to bring the coat I left with Carpus at Troas. Also bring my books, and especially my papers. [14] Alexander the coppersmith did me much harm, but the Lord will judge him for what he has done. [15] Be careful of him, for he fought against everything we said. [16] The first time I was brought before the judge, no one came with me. Everyone abandoned me. May it not be counted against them. [17] But the Lord stood with me and gave me strength so that I might preach the Good News in its entirety for all the Gentiles to hear. And he rescued me from certain death. [18] Yes, and the Lord will deliver me from every evil attack and will bring me safely into his heavenly Kingdom. All glory to God forever and ever! Amen. [19] Give my greetings to Priscilla and Aquila and those living in the household of Onesiphorus. [20] Erastus stayed at Corinth, and I left Trophimus sick at Miletus. [21]

Do your best to get here before winter. Eubulus sends you greetings, and so do Pudens, Linus, Claudia, and all the brothers and sisters. [22] May the Lord be with your spirit. And may his grace be with all of you. (TLB)

Stop listening to what you are being told and use the talent that God has given you. Stop letting your belief in God be determined by those who don't want a God in their lives or have dictated the way that you should believe. Read for yourself. God is calling! Do you have the faith to answer?

10
MY PSALMS

ONE OF THE "side effects" of having my story told is haiku's. Under the influence of Terry Smith, I started writing poetry. Weird! I hated poetry when I was in college. Now I write them every now and then. Terry writes Haikus about his life and Grace. His writing is an answer to God and what he is reading from the scripture. From there I thought "hey, I can do this". There was some research done and soon I was writing my own poems. I call these my psalms. Some are written when I was low and others were written when things are going well. You will see the main influence in my life. May you enjoy these.

MY PSALMS

This is the first of my poems. It is the start of my writing. This poem was written just after my Mom died.

THE JOURNEY

This day a journey made...
The Departure:
Anxious,
    Apprehension,
        Foreboding,
            Solicitude,
                Uncertainty,

You see this journey is like no other,
It is the first trip home without my Mother.

the arrival:
Hugs,
    Love,
        Peace,
            Warmth,
                Assurance,
                    Contentment.

The return:
Hugs,
    Love (purrs),
        Peace,
            Warmth,
                Assurance,
                    Contentment.

As I think back and reflect on how it went
I can positively say things are the same, just different.

A Prayer For Inner Peace

Tears are shed
While each prayer is said
My soul cries out
Longing for an answer

The pain surrounds me
"Is there a God?" I ask
If so, why must I suffer?
If he cares, why the torment?

The questions come from all sides
Once a belief, now a doubt
Undeserved is this I thought
Eli, Eli lama sabacthani!

Anger at God
He must be to blame
Why let this happen?
If his commands control all things?

CAUGHT IN THE MIDDLE

Time passes and gives way
Rational thinking, the answer is realized
God has thick shins
He expects a reaction.

Man is to blame, not God.
It started in the garden
And ended in shame
Separation and death resulted

Wandering, alone, and lost
Then came Immanuel
Love he shared
Death he conquered

On Earth, our struggles continue
True peace cannot be realized
Satan, like "the bird" from a certain movie, daily batters
The suffering seems endless

MY PSALMS

Physically, mentally, spiritually
The challenges come
Very few will have the strength to stand
Faith to hold the cross above one's head

Knowing one day Jesus will return
And victory shall be won
For on that day into Heaven
We shall all be led

This haiku is a brief synopsis of a dark time in my life.

Chosen

A word used on occasion
For a team
For a project
For a position

One can be chosen by an animal
For me it is a cat
A soft, yellow tabby friend
Gigi is her name

"Baker girl" is her alias
Biscuits she loves to make
A soft meow
A gentle purr

A constant companion
She walks with me
She talks with me
She longs to be everywhere I am

MY PSALMS

We are chosen by God
We are his people
Like a branch
We have been grafted in

It started as a few
Now it is for all
Beginning in Peter's vision
Then continuing through Paul

A relational love that exists
It quenches all thirst
It fills all hunger
Mercy he continually shows

As a hen gathers her chicks
So he wishes to do for us.
He has made his choice
All we need is to reciprocate

CAUGHT IN THE MIDDLE

For God so loved us
That he gave his ONLY son
That whomever believes in him
Shall not perish but have eternal life.

This is my 3rd haiku. It speaks for itself.

Feral Cats, Feral Souls

Alone and lost
Each day is a trial
Darwinism is the way
Only the strong survive

Daily food is a struggle
Sometimes it is in your trash
Other times you see me beg
There are many days I go without

Sleep comes as needed
Exposed to the elements
Finding a safe place to lay my head
Each close of my eyes could be my last

Along comes a stranger
They call me to befriend me
I do not trust the hand that offers
But hunger is the motivating factor

Eventually I approach

CAUGHT IN THE MIDDLE

Food is given
Trust builds with passage
After time and constant love

Eventually I see what can be
Plenty of nourishment
Toys with which to play
A safe place to rest

For so much time
I resisted and fought
Not knowing the peace
Made possible through love

The same can be said with humans
Who live in a world full of sin
Darkness covers the land
Whether good or bad, it is the same

We long for acceptance
Making bad choices along the way
A short term fix is the answer
That buries us further in pain

MY PSALMS

Alone and lost
Each day is a trial
Darwinism is the way
Only the strong survive

Along comes a stranger
Sits by me at the well
Looks up at me in a tree
Shows love and comes to eat with me

The call is there
I just have to listen
He opens my life up
A better way is offered

A choice is given
Struggling with life
My way or the highway
Or his way with peace

Like a hen that covers her chicks
So he pursues us

CAUGHT IN THE MIDDLE

Every sparrow known
Every hair counted

A place of rest
Unlimited nourishment
Constant companionship
An end to sickness and death

Many mansions have been built
A new Heaven and a new Earth
All I have to do is choose
Outstretched is the hand

I work with stray cats. I learn lessons from my work. Sometimes my work and spirituality mix.

Ratio Of Love

They say it's 50/50
Others say 100/100
That make a successful
Relationship that lasts

Those are worldly terms
Good in their own respect
But Jesus gives his own version
Of healthy comradeship

He tells the story of sheep
Where one is lost
The shepherd leaves 99
To look for the one

A celebration ensues
Just for the one that is found
Love unbounded
A different way is shown

CAUGHT IN THE MIDDLE

It defies logic
A mystery to be sure
The needs of the one
Outweigh the needs of the many

So now we know the ratio
Real love is given
To those needs of the other
More than our wants

I tell my kids often
How much they are loved
The real number is shared
The ratio given by Jesus

To having a lasting love
The same as he has for us
Both parties need this in mind
The ratio of love is 1 to 99

Memories

The bed
The toy
The little dish
All serve as reminders

The morning is the worst
Everyone comes to eat
No longer her
The tears flow

After every loss
An empty place exists
The heart hurts
Memories are around

An earthquake has happened
Shaken our soul
A hole is created
Love must fill

CAUGHT IN THE MIDDLE

Christ is that love
He was the example
Fruits of the spirit
Need to rule our lives

Be fruitful
And multiply
That is the saying
We need to live by

He had no toy, no dish
The Son of Man
He had no place
To lay his head

How do we remember
God on earth
We (humans) killed his son
A literal earthquake followed

Each act of kindness
Done here on earth

MY PSALMS

Is a reminder of Christ
This is how God remembers

Every naked person clothed
Every sick person visited
Every person in prison seen
Remaining unstained by the world

Love God
Love others
The only two commands
He gave throughout the Bible

These are the memories
That God has of Christ
Each kind deed we do
Brings feelings of happiness

Thoughts on my head as I wrestle with the loss of Midas, my cat. Other references come from Matthew 8:20, Luke 9:58, Matthew 25:36, and James 1:27. Let us make happy memories.

A Tribute To Dad

How does one say goodbye
This is a permanent parting
A period when your time
In this world is near it's end

If it is a surprise
Or if it is known
Does not make a difference
The hurt is still the same

The memories come flooding
The chess games
The numbered sermons
The list goes on and on

The make-up jobs
The many trips
homework at a politician's house
And, of course, the spankings

MY PSALMS

He instilled right and wrong
Virtues that are rarely seen
Even our religion has changed
What was wrong now is right

Things never change with Dad
He reflects God in all things
Many conversations are had
Always there is Bible mentioned

Most of all the thing on top
The times that should be trouble
Instead they were easy
Grace was shown like God

It is given freely
Something we don't deserve
He fought for us as young ones
Now the battle is his to fight

Although his days are numbered
I want him to know

CAUGHT IN THE MIDDLE

He will eternally be in my heart
Till I see him in the next age

You have done a fine job
All things that I accomplish
Will be a tribute
For YOU are my Dad

Your son, Brice

This was read to my father as he laid in a hospice facility.

ABOUT THE AUTHOR

Jack Brice Medlin, II is a chef, food designer, problem solver, and cat lover. This is his first book and he plans to follow with others.

For years, Jack has lived his own life. Then he discovered that someone else needed to be in charge. Looking back, he sees that God helped him all along the way.

Jack is an entrepreneur. He is starting several businesses. His companies include The Cat Dude, Music City Smoked Cheesecake, and Eden Hooks. He is a failed foster and currently has 4 cats.

ABOUT THE PUBLISHER

Kary Oberbrunner and David Branderhorst started Author Academy Elite in 2014 rather by accident. Their clients kept asking for a program to help them write, publish, and market their books the right way. After months of resisting, they shared a new publishing paradigm one evening in March on a call. They had nothing built and knew it would take six months to implement that idea and create a premium experience.

Regardless of the unknowns, twenty-five aspiring authors jumped in immediately, and Author Academy Elite was born. Today Author Academy

Elite attracts hundreds of quality authors who share a mutual commitment to create vibrant businesses around their books. Discover more about the model at AuthorAcademyElite.com.

Truth Seekers

DO YOU WANT TO BE A PART OF A GROUP THAT IS SEARCHING FOR THE HEART OF CHRIST?

Join the Truth Seekers group for a small fee. This is a private group of individuals that come together to find the truth. Be one today!

Truth Seekers

JBM

JACK BRICE MEDLIN II

see a place to get this book and more
available at the following website

4JBooks.com

CPSIA information can be obtained
at www.ICGtesting.com
Printed in the USA
LVHW032232190620
658514LV00005B/5

9 781647 461942